For more information, please visit *gestalten.com*

———

Bibliographic information published by the Deutsche Nationalbibliothek: The Deutsche Nationalbibliothek lists this publication in the Deutsche Nationalbibliografie; detailed bibliographic data are available online at *dnb.d-nb.de*

MIX
Paper from responsible sources
FSC
www.fsc.org   FSC® C011712

This book was printed on paper certified by the FSC®

Monocle editor in chief and chairman: *Tyler Brûlé*
Monocle editor: *Andrew Tuck*
Books editor: *Joe Pickard*
Guide editor: *Chloë Ashby*

———

Designed by *Monocle*
Proofreading by *Monocle*
Typeset in *Plantin & Helvetica*

———

Printed by *Offsetdruckerei Grammlich, Pliezhausen*

Made in Germany

Published by *gestalten*, Berlin 2019
ISBN 978-3-89955-973-6

© Die Gestalten Verlag GmbH & Co. KG, Berlin 2019

The MONOCLE
Travel Guide Series

Brussels +
Antwerp

Contents
—— Brussels + Antwerp

Use the key below to
help navigate the guide
section by section.

 H Hotels

F Food and drink

R Retail

C Culture

D Design and architecture

S Sport and fitness

W Walks

B Best of the rest

T Things we'd buy

E Essays

Antwerp

Brussels

Salut! Join us as we capture our favourite places in the Belgian capital. Snap to it!

Welcome
—— Bonjour
Brussels

As the host of the *European Union* institutions (and the Nato headquarters), "Brussels" has become shorthand for the EU. But there's much more to the Belgian capital than politics. It has plenty to offer visitors in town for business or pleasure, from *art nouveau architecture* to independent boutiques. It's peppered with *leafy parks* and, though Belgian cuisine may not be at the top of everyone's dining bucket list, it's also brimming with first-rate restaurants.

Belgium ranks highly on the global scale of Michelin stars per capita but thankfully it isn't all white tablecloths and tasting menus – instead you'll find *jazzy bars*, *breezy bistros* and a *bubbling coffee culture*. Commercial galleries brush shoulders with institutions dedicated to late greats such as *René Magritte* (pipe included) and the city finally has a landmark contemporary-art museum – Kanal-Centre Pompidou, a joint venture between the City of Brussels and the Pompidou in Paris.

Admittedly for a capital city, Brussels is short on top-tier hotels. But with the next generation making waves across sectors from culture to hospitality, that's sure to change.

Brussels is at once *local and global*, rooted in Belgian tradition while keeping an eye on what's going on around the world. It's the kind of place that keeps things close to its chest; you'll need a steer on where to go so allow us to introduce you. You'll soon see that, behind closed doors, this capital city has bags of charm to spare. — (M)

Map

—— Bird's-eye Brussels

Navigating Brussels couldn't be simpler. In the city centre you'll find all the postcard attractions: Grand Place, the royal palaces and the infamous Manneken Pis statue. To the east, in the Quartier Européen, are the headquarters of the EU plus hundreds of companies operating in the political sphere (this is also where you'll find the historic townhouses that recall the Brussels of old).

Southeast is a cluster of neighbourhoods, such as Saint-Gilles and Flagey, that we would recommend above all: think art nouveau architecture, top restaurants, lively bars and a local crowd. (Note that the Bruxellois often refer to this part of town as Ixelles, though that name actually refers to a huge district that covers a far greater area.) And just beyond these comely streets is the sprawling Bois de la Cambre, a forest-like park that is the lungs of the city.

Northwest of the centre is Molenbeek, villainised in the press as a hotbed of unrest but in fact a hub for parties, art collectives and cultural diversity. And further north you'll find Laeken, home to a large park, the royal residence and the Atomium.

QUARTIER MARITIME

QUARTIER NORD

MOLENBEEK HISTORIQUE

BÉGUINAGE

DANSAERT

Mima

Grand Place

ANNEESSENS

GRAND PLACE

STALINGRAD

CUREGHEM

SABLO

MAROLLES

Bruxelles-Midi

Palais de Justi

GARE DU MIDI

PORTE DE HAL

HÔTEL DES MONNAIES

HAUT SAINT-GILLES

Musée Hor

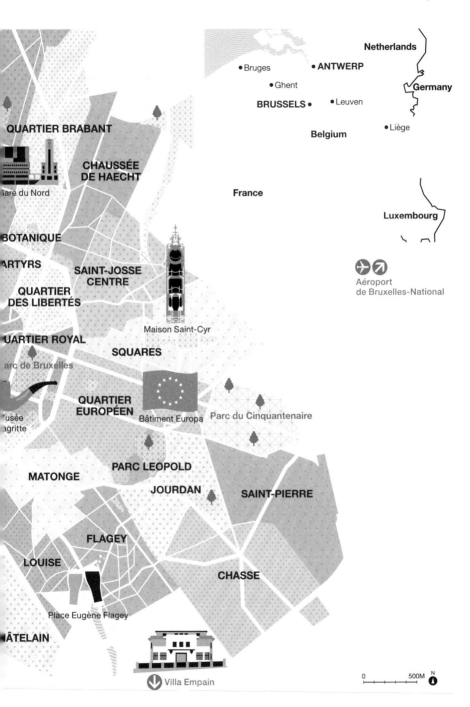

Brussels Map

Netherlands

Bruges

ANTWERP

Ghent

BRUSSELS

Leuven

Germany

Liège

Belgium

France

Luxembourg

Aéroport
de Bruxelles-National

QUARTIER BRABANT

CHAUSSÉE
DE HAECHT

Gare du Nord

BOTANIQUE

ARTYRS

SAINT-JOSSE
CENTRE

QUARTIER
DES LIBERTÉS

Maison Saint-Cyr

UARTIER ROYAL

arc de Bruxelles

SQUARES

usée
agritte

QUARTIER
EUROPÉEN

Bâtiment Europa

Parc du Cinquantenaire

PARC LEOPOLD

MATONGE

JOURDAN

SAINT-PIERRE

FLAGEY

LOUISE

CHASSE

Place Eugène Flagey

ÂTELAIN

Villa Empain

0   500M   N

011

Need to know
— Bite-sized Brussels

The European Union
Key player

Brussels is the de facto HQ of the European Union (there is no "official" headquarters). The reason? By the time the Treaties of Rome were signed on 25 March 1957 – creating the European Economic Community and the European Atomic Energy Community, and thereby laying the cornerstones of the EU community – there was still no consensus as to which city from the six signatory nations would host the union's functionaries. As a provisional solution, the group decided that the host would rotate in alphabetical order: Belgium was up first. From then on it became a question of habit – Brussels proved an apt host – until July 2004, when it was formally agreed that the Belgian capital should always be the host of the four regular meetings of the EU heads of government.

When in Brussels....

Getting around
On the right track

Brussels' relatively central location makes it quick and easy to explore the rest of Belgium. Antwerp and Bruges are under an hour away from Bruxelles-Midi by train, Ghent 30 minutes. And if you fancy hopping across the border, Amsterdam is a cool two hours away by train.

History
Back-in-the-day Belgium

Belgium became an independent state in 1831 when southern provinces of the newly minted Kingdom of the Netherlands seceded. Europe's global powers, such as the British Empire, mediated in the conflict and suggested a German prince called Leopold – with no ties to Belgium at all – as king. His dynasty continues to rule the country today.

No one suspected that Belgium would ever have the oomph to make it big in Europe but the little state was the second country to industrialise after Britain and became one of the richest nations in the world – though this was in greater part achieved by the brutal exploitation of Congo starting in the 1870s.

The First and Second World Wars devastated the country and depleted the coffers. But in the second half of the 20th century, Belgium's luck turned for the better: it helped found the EU and Nato. Indeed, this period of its history has become synonymous with the beginning of some of the world's most important political institutions.

Language divide
Talk the talk

What language does the Belgian football team communicate in? English. That's because Belgium is split into the Dutch-speaking Flemish side in the north and the French-speaking Walloon side to the south. (Though Brussels is marketed as bilingual, generally it's French-speaking). As such it's not uncommon to find two Belgians struggling to communicate.

Though sometimes this linguistic-cultural divide does swell into animosity, generally it's looked at as a benign and quirky – though impractical – part of Belgian heritage (*see page 128*).

Beer
Cheers to that

Beer to Belgium is what wine is to France. The brewing tradition here goes back almost a millennium and in 2016 was added to Unesco's "list of the intangible cultural heritage of humanity".

There are hundreds of breweries across the country producing a breadth of beers, from light and refreshing lager-like tipples to deep, dark and sweet variants that go straight to the head. (Make sure you check the strength of the drink you're ordering: 8 to 10 per cent is quite normal; some reach up to 20 per cent.) The most prestigious output of this tradition is Trappist beer, brewed seasonally across six monasteries by monks of the Order of Cistercians of the Strict Observance.

Brusselisation
Poor planning

The concept is as ugly as the word: Brusselisation is the wanton introduction of modern architecture (not the good kind) and high-rises into a city. After the Second World War, Brussels put excessive faith in the promise of modern architecture to the detriment of its historic cityscape. And what with the frantic preparations for the 1958 World Expo, the government tore down building after building to make way for gleaming new structures in the hope of impressing the influx of visitors.

All of the above was done with inadequate planning, and the result is the eyesore we have today. Thankfully neighbourhoods outside the central ring road – such as Saint-Gilles, Flagey and Squares – are relatively untouched and still carry the spirit of old Brussels.

Office hours
Travelling circus

Brussels is home to a huge number of international institutions and companies. Like the EU offices, these are in full swing during the week but go quiet at the weekend, which explains why hotel prices tend to rocket – sometimes up to five times their regular value – on weekdays. If you're planning a trip, keep an eye on the dates and find out if there are any big political or corporate events in town: it could mean the difference between a charming break and a costly one stuck in traffic behind sirens and diplomatic number plates.

Developing the city
Grow with the flow

Brussels is growing. Laeken – home to an eclectic bunch including the Royal Castle, the Atomium and Mini-Europe – is slated to be developed into a vast mixed-used neighbourhood by 2027. NEO project is one of the city's flagship undertakings and the government is confident that it will rejuvenate the area, which is currently a tourist trap. Hopefully it won't be a case of Brusselisation (see left).

If I fly under that, does that make me subatomic?

Food
Plate expectations

It's an ongoing joke that Belgians only eat waffles, mussels, frites and chocolate. Naturally you'll find oodles of all four – and do note that frites are a Belgian invention, not French – but this country's gastronomic pedigree is more nuanced than you'd expect.

Dabble in the free chocolate samples by Grand Place, by all means, but also check out the inventive chefs leading the charge in Brussels (see pages 20 to 31). There's a serious movement putting emphasis on fresh seafood and locally sourced fruit, vegetables, meat and game. There's also plenty to cater for international palates, from no-frills Syrian to some of the best pizza this side of the Alps.

Our top picks:

01 Hotel des Galeries: A pad paying homage to contemporary art and design. *see pages 14-15*
02 Belga & Co: Sip coffee in this cosy café or its leafy back garden. *see page 29*
03 Wiels: Rotating exhibitions by emerging and established artists. *see page 42*
04 Chez Richard: French and Belgian classics, plus a punchy wine list. *see page 27*
05 Le Typographe: A top-draw stationery-maker in a narrow townhouse. *see pages 38-39*
06 Palais des Beaux-Arts: Leading, and largely subterranean, cultural centre. *see page 46*
07 Musée Horta: Make a beeline for the former home of the art nouveau pioneer. *see page 56*
08 La Buvette: Vegetable-centric tasting menus made with the pick of the market. *see page 21*
09 Eva Velazquez: Charming womenswear shop selling unique, long-lasting pieces. *see page 32*
10 Villa Empain: Art deco meets Bauhaus at this imposing villa. *see pages 54-55*

(Surely one of these languages will work!)

Hallo Bonjour

Hotels
—— Get a room

①
Hotel des Galeries, Grand Place
Designer digs

For a city brimming with business, good food and first-class cultural offerings, it's baffling that Brussels' hotel scene isn't more forward thinking. It's not that there's a dearth of options, just that most are somewhat middle-of-the-road. The city also has a strange affinity for themed stays that err on the side of gimmickry.

But don't worry – we've found a handful of hotels that offer the best of both old and new Brussels. Design aficionados will delight in the light and airy rooms offered by a prominent Parisian publisher (plenty of reading material included), while art-history buffs will revel at the opportunity to bed down in the former home of one of the world's most pre-eminent neoclassical painters.

The capital of EU bureaucracy hums with suited guests during the week, while at the weekend those in search of a charming city break check in. Whenever you visit, the following hotels will make fine bases from which to explore the city.

The historic Galeries Royales Saint-Hubert may recall times past but the hotel located at their centre pays homage to contemporary art and design. Opened in 2014 by Parisian publisher and art collector Nadine Flammarion, and laid out by her daughter Camille together with interior designer Fleur Delesalle, the Hotel des Galeries has raised the bar for hotels in Brussels.

Spread across four floors, each of the 20 rooms and three suites retains the former shopping arcade's parquet floors and shuttered windows. White walls are pepped up with vibrant prints by 20th and 21st-century artists such as Sonia Delaunay, the colours of which are picked out in rugs, cushions and other design details. Furniture by Belgian designers including Sylvain Willenz sits alongside antiques picked up in the Sablon neighbourhood, while books by Flammarion and ceramics made by Camille are dotted around the hotel.
38 Rue des Bouchers, 1000
+ 32 (0)2 213 7470
hoteldesgaleries.be

MONOCLE COMMENT: Don't miss Daniel Buren's Plexiglas artwork in the lounge, from Camille's private collection.

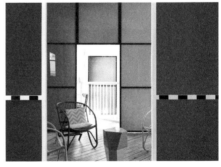

38, 37, 36, 35, 34 → 3 → 33, 32, 31

②

Pillows Grand Hotel Place
Rouppe, Stalingrad
Refined all-rounder

This tasteful hotel by Dutch
hospitality team IHMG delivers
43 rooms that would suit a
weekend getaway and work
trip alike. The informal ground
floor – where the lounge,
reception and restaurant-bar
(boasting a magnificent marble
island) blend into one – sets
the tone. It's all muted shades,
abstract art and Carl Hansen
& Søn chairs, courtesy of
Amsterdam-based interior
architects Studio Linse.

We recommend a room
overlooking Place Rouppe for
maximum sunlight but don't
be deterred by the lowest,
"Luxury", category: even these
are unabashedly spacious.
17 Place Rouppe, 1000
+ 32 (0)2 204 0040
pillowshotels.com/brussels

MONOCLE COMMENT:
On check in, do take the
complimentary welcome drink
and gather around the fire
before heading upstairs. And
if you're yet to make dinner
plans, consider the in-house
restaurant run by chef Trung
Hoang (*pictured*).

③
Jardin Secret, Matonge
Hidden surprise

One of four Brussels boltholes in the Limited Edition Hotels stable, Jardin Secret is tucked away on a cobbled street in Matonge. As the name implies, there's a secret garden at its centre, and greenery features throughout, with pot plants and cacti perched on shelves in the reception and a leafy ceiling in the restaurant (which is shared with the next-door Hotel Le Berger). Landscape designer and gardener Claire Van der Schueren checks in on her horticultural creations monthly.

Designed by Belgian architect Olivia Gustot, the hotel opened in 2017. The 33 rooms vary in shape and size but the decor is consistent: white bed linen, stone-coloured blankets, patterned cushions plus wicker chairs and reed mats from Morocco. Each room has a writing desk and offers total quiet – apart from the trickling of the fountain.
22 Rue du Berger, 1050
+32 (0)2 510 8349
jardinsecrethotel.be

Maybe trying to steal a cactus is a bad idea

MONOCLE COMMENT: Opt for a ground-floor room if you fancy lashings of light and a good garden view. If you're with family or friends, there are larger rooms for four or five; it may be a squeeze but some come with two bathrooms.

4

Hotel Le Dixseptième,
Grand Place
Listed beauty

This grande dame sits in a
Unesco World Heritage site
in the city centre. The original
building was erected on
Brussels' first paved road in
the 14th century and partially
rebuilt three centuries later
after Louis XIV bombarded
the city in 1695. The 17th-
century timber rooftop,
curved staircase and stone
reliefs remain.

The 37 rooms are divided
into three categories – Classic,
Patio and Garden – as well
as three buildings. The Garden
rooms are the most recently
built but, if you're after
something a little different,
we'd suggest one of the more
spacious Classics – some
boasting open fireplaces, others
a private terrace. Each room is
named after a Belgian painter
and decorated accordingly.
*25 Rue de la Madeleine, 1000
+32 (0)2 517 1717
ledixseptieme.be*

MONOCLE COMMENT: With
three meeting rooms, a fitness
centre and a sauna, Hotel Le
Dixseptième is suitable for
someone in town on business.

Dependable chains

01 The Dominican, Grand
Place: The Brussels
outpost of the Carlton
Hotel Collection is in
a former 15th-century
Dominican abbey,
once also the home
of neoclassical painter
Jacques-Louis David.
Hang your hat in one of
150 rooms, then unwind
in the Finnish sauna or
Turkish steam bath.
*carlton.nl/en/the-
dominican-hotel-brussels*

02 Brussels Marriott Hotel
Grand Place, Dansaert:
This city-centre bolthole
is ideal for a quick work
trip, featuring simple
rooms with ample space
to work, plus seven
sizeable meeting rooms.
*marriott.co.uk/hotels/
travel/brudt-brussels-
marriott-hotel-grand-
place*

03 Hotel Amigo, Grand
Place: This stay by Rocco
Forte Hotels offers a
combination of traditional
and modern rooms by
design director Olga
Polizzi. For added luxury,
opt for a suite peppered
with art by contemporary
Belgian artists.
*roccofortehotels.com/
hotels-and-resorts/
hotel-amigo*

Encore, encore
———
In a 1930s modernist
building in Dansaert are three
apartments from the owners
of Alice Gallery (*see page 44*).
Fitted with furniture by Ateliers
J&J and artwork sourced by
Alice Gallery, they're available
for short and long-term rent.
encorebrussels.com

Food and drink
—— Fare with flair

For a city closely associated with beige foodstuffs, Brussels packs a surprising culinary punch. Due respect should certainly be given to the holy trinity of frites, beer and waffles – but there's so much more besides.

Handsome art nouveau buildings and affordable rents have attracted plucky young chefs from France and further afield who have jumped at the chance to showcase their talents in playful, intimate settings. "There's a sense," says Nicolas Scheidt of La Buvette, "that here in Brussels things are possible."

That's not to say that traditional cuisine isn't worth a try: thanks to a growing interest in organic farming and the city's proximity to the coast, hearty Belgian classics are a treat too. A cut-throat dining scene this isn't, so expect many restaurants to close on Sundays or Mondays. Brunch has picked up speed over the past few years but check ahead as many spots only offer it one day a week. And for all those hours in between? A visit to a *friterie*, brewery or waffle truck never goes amiss.

Dinner
Where to eat

①
Le Bout de Gras, Châtelain
Spirited bistro

Born in Réunion and trained in Belgium by a Japanese chef, Laurent Balancy (*pictured*) channels his international spirit at this lively bistro. Think classic French dishes with a Creole twist, such as a signature cassoulet spiked with turmeric leaves and garlic.

Balancy's nose-to-tail approach and expert way with a whole fish has earned him many fans. Regulars often turn up for lunch and stay until dinner, working their way through microbrewed suds and easy-to-quaff bottles of natural wine.
*89 Rue Américaine, 1050
+ 32 (0)488 160 012
leboutdegras.be*

2
La Buvette, Haut Saint-Gilles
French fancy

Once an extension of Café des Spores across the road, this former butcher shop is now a dining destination in its own right. A considered conversion by Lhoas & Lhoas has kept the venue's decorative quirks and casual elegance.

Self-taught Alsace chef Nicolas Scheidt runs the kitchen, whipping up vegetable-centric tasting menus based on whatever looks good at the market. He's proud, too, of the organic bread from sister bakery Hopla Geiss, the third jewel in his budding emporium.
108 Chaussée d'Alsemberg, 1060
+ 32 (0)2 534 1303
la-buvette.be

One
for
you,
five
for me

③
Le Vismet, Béguinage
Sea-fresh

Set in a typical Flemish red-brick house, Le Vismet takes its name from the fish market that once stood nearby. No prizes for guessing the house speciality then: this paean to seafood is a Brussels institution.

Its classic approach – tables draped in white linen, nature illustrations on the walls – is tempered by a modern open kitchen and relaxed but courteous service. The seafood platter is a must, stacked with crab claws, Normandy oysters and sweet crustaceans. The rest of the fuss-free menu covers all-time favourites, from tuna tartare and sole meunière to pollack fillets with hand-peeled Ostend prawns.
23 Place Sainte-Catherine, 1000
+ 32 (0)2 218 8545
levismet.be

④
Le Petit Racines, Flagey
Pasta, pronto

If you've left it too late to get a table at gourmet haunt Racines, drop by its little sibling next door. Italian owners Ugo Federico and Francesco Cury (*both pictured, Cury on left*) wanted to start an easy-on-the-wallet neighbourhood joint where locals could pop in for a spritz and snack on chickpea crêpes or grilled scamorza cheese.

Pasta is made from scratch every day (Federico still gets stuck in) and served speedily with slow-cooked sauces: a Puglian lamb ragù, say, or a peppy puttanesca. You could be in and out the door in half an hour but you'd do yourself a disservice not to linger over the tiramisu.
347 Chaussée d'Ixelles, 1050
+ 32 (0)2 633 4303
racinesbruxelles.com

⑤
Chez Léon, Grand Place
Mussels in Brussels

Léon Vanlancker's humble *moules-frites* joint has come a long way since it opened here more than 125 years ago. The same family still runs it, though it now sprawls through nine slender townhouses, plus a more intimate cobblestoned terrace.

In spite of its tourist-trap location just off Grand Place, Chez Léon is popular with locals for the plumpness of its Zealand mussels, in season from July to March. Choose to have them steamed with celery, onion and butter, given the lardon or curry treatment, or grilled with garlic, cheese or tomato. You'd be remiss to try anything else.
18 Rue des Bouchers, 1000
+32 (0)2 511 1415
chezleon.be

Must-try
Meatballs from Ballekes, Grand Place
The *boulette* (meatball) ignites regional passions and goes by many names: *vitoulet* in Charleroi or *boulet* in Liège. Mini-chain Ballekes gives them a modern spin – spiked with chicory or beer – but they're at their most moreish in tomato sauce.
ballekes.be

6
Le 203, Haut Saint-Gilles
Fine fusion

An evening at this Haut
Saint-Gilles hit, run by
globe-trotting owners Richard
Schaffer and Mathilde Hatte,
feels a bit like a relaxed dinner
party at a friend's house.
The tight menu, scrawled
on a wall-mounted paper roll,
spans a couple of starters,
mains and desserts, the
daily fruit of chef Schaffer's
imagination. He earned his
stripes in Vietnam, South
Africa and Australia, so expect
tantalising fusion fare laced
with fragrant herbs and spices.
    Arguably the best seats in
the house are at the kitchen
counter or in the leafy garden
in fine weather; both welcome
guests without a booking, if
you're in town last minute.
203 Chaussée de Waterloo, 1060
+ 32 (0)2 539 2643
le203.com

⑦
Cocina, Flagey
Dolce vita

Cocina has a Neapolitan buzz,
though the decor – rough-hewn
wooden tables, exposed-brick
walls and Carrara marble
counter – has more than a whiff
of Brooklyn about it. Shipped
over from Naples, a big wood-
fired oven takes centre stage,
churning out pitch-perfect
pizzas from slow-risen dough.
Toppings are everything you'd
hope for: Sicilian aubergines,
smoked ricotta, black-truffle
shavings and more.
    Cocktails play the Italian
card too, from classic spritzes
to Negronis. It's popular so
there may be a wait – but
that's no hardship when you're
propping up the bar. A second
outpost in Châtelain specialises
in pasta.
16 Rue Lesbroussart, 1050
+ 32 (0)2 644 9400
cocina.be

8
Tero, Hôtel des Monnaies
Earthly pleasures

Healthy, colourful fare stars
at this small-plates restaurant,
which takes farm-to-table
eating very seriously. Much
of its produce comes from
the Ferme des Rabanisse, an
organic estate where grass-fed
cows and free-range pigs are
raised ethically.
    Working with the seasons,
founder Arthur Lhoist treats
this bounty with respect and
a sense of adventure. And in
a city packed with intimate
townhouse restaurants, the
airy, minimalist setting is a
pleasant change of scene.
1 Rue Saint-Bernard, 1060
+ 32 (0)2 347 7946
tero-restaurant.com

Local institutions

At heart, the Belgian capital is a creature of habit. Blessed with art nouveau settings and legendary recipes, these venues have changed little over the years.

01 **Maison Dandoy, Grand Place:** This tearoom serves more than *speculoos* (spiced biscuits). No sides are taken in the Brussels versus Liège waffle conflict, so try both. *maisondandoy.com*

02 **Au Vieux Saint Martin, Sablon:** Antiques dealers, ladies in furs and star patissier Pierre Marcolini rub shoulders here. Come for coffee or a cocktail. *auvieuxsaintmartin.be*

03 **Bonnefooi, Grand Place:** This haunt stays open until it's time for a restorative breakfast. There's music most nights, a mezzanine for strutting and dark corners for more intimate chats. *bonnefooi.be*

04 **Le Cirio, Grand Place:** Coiffed Bruxellois visit for a half-and-half (the house mix of still and sparkling wines) and a glimpse of Chocolat, the diamanté-collared cat. *18 Rue de la Bourse, 1000*

Fried and tested

In spite of a notoriously bad-tempered owner and painfully slow queues, fans still make the pilgrimage to old-school *friterie* Frit Flagey. It's a tribute to the golden perfection of its frites, twice-cooked in beef fat and topped with creamy mayo. *Place Eugène Flagey, 1050*

Lunch
On the trot

Must-try
Prawn croquettes from Fernand Obb, Haut Saint-Gilles
There's a trick to eating these like a local: cut them lengthwise to avoid scalding yourself with volcanic béchamel. Crispy, creamy and served on a bed of fried parsley, the Fernand Obb kind are the best in town. *fernand-obb.be*

①
Knees to Chin, Dansaert
Street style

A world away from croquettes and *carbonnades* (Flemish beef stew), the flavour-packed summer rolls by Roxane and Agathe Gernacrt (*both pictured, Roxane on left*) are served in three spaces across the city. The concept is simple: a menu of eight rice rolls marrying crunchy vegetables with the likes of duck or aubergine.

Hanoi this isn't but the result is both healthy and delicious. Each roll comes with a sauce and you're free to mix and match with four other zingy options, provided in squeezy bottles. If you can't find a seat in the diminutive dining room, there's a bench outside on Place Sainte-Catherine to savour your spoils.
28 Rue de Flandre, 1000
+ 32 (0)2 503 1831
kneestochin.com

Target locked. Engage

2
My Tannour, Flagey
Bun in the oven

The name says it all. *Tannour*
is a typical Syrian flatbread –
charred here and there, with
little air pockets. It's the starting
point of any good Syrian meal
and the heart of this no-frills,
sleeves-up operation.

Owner Georges Baghdi Sar,
born to Armenian-Lebanese
parents in Syria, stands behind
the red-clay oven most days
baking the good stuff and
welcoming hungry customers
with a smile. On offer are
delightfully simple variations
of falafel, halloumi or various
meats with grilled vegetables,
dips and the obligatory *tannour*.
Queue to order at the counter,
grab a cold IPA from the fridge
and find a table.
98 Rue de la Brasserie, 1050
+ 32 (0)471 451 600

Vintage treasure

On Place du Jeu de Balle,
La Brocante's terrace has front-
row seats to the flea market's
wheeling and dealing. Bargain-
hunting calls for hearty comfort
food: bolognese toast and
omelettes, plus tart Gueuze
beers and live jazz on Sundays.
cafelabrocante.skyrock.com

③
Chez Richard, Sablon
Bistro à la cool

Sadri Rokbani, Mallory Saussus, Thomas Kok and Fanny Schenkel already had a couple of happening cafés under their belt when they took on the task of renovating this bijou bistro. Parisian designer Nicolas Hannequin dreamed up the rose-and-electric-blue palette, echoed in the laid-back staff's natty jumpers.

The menu is equally relaxed – a timeless mix of French and Belgian classics rustled up from quality ingredients. The cured-ham croque monsieur comes in a generous double portion that's big enough for two. The wine list is also a crowd-pleaser, with French and Italian vintages alongside biodynamic bottles.
2 Rue des Minimes, 1000
+ 32 (0)479 611 256
chezrichard.be

④
Noordzee, Dansaert
Fresh off the boat

There's no shortage of great seafood spots in town, thanks to a steady supply from the nearby coast. Noordzee (La Mer du Nord, in French) trumps them all, and routinely outshines its competitor ABC Poissonnerie across the road.

The fish counter is excellent but it's long been eclipsed by the sleek cooked-to-order operation. Take your pick from the day's catch – whelks, whitebait or razor clams, say, scrawled haphazardly on a whiteboard – then decamp to the nearest standing table with a bottle of something crisp and cold. Listen to the sizzle of grills and hot oil and, when your name is hollered, you know you're in for a treat.
45 Place Sainte-Catherine, 1000
+ 32 (0)2 513 1192
noordzeemerdunord.be

Killer fillers

Don't be alarmed by the *pistolets* (literally "pistols") sold in cafés and takeaway stalls across town. These traditional sandwiches, made with round and crusty bread rolls, owe their name more to medieval coins (or possibly bakers, the etymology is hazy) than firearms. Brussels is experimental when it comes to fillings so approach lunch with an adventurous spirit.

01   Pistolet Original, Sablon: Owner Valérie Lepla champions local produce and proud Belgian classics. Options include *Américain* (beef tartare) garnished with cress or black pudding set in sauerkraut steeped in Cantillon beer.
pistolet-original.be

02   Maison Antoine, Jourdan: Upgrade to a *mitraillette* (machine gun) at this frying hut that's been going since 1948. Meaty baguettes (merguez sausage and pork satay, for example) are topped with frites hot from the fryer and your pick of more than 30 sauces.
maisonantoine.be

03   Tonton Garby, Grand Place: Arm yourself with a little patience at this hole in the wall, where queuing can stretch to 40 minutes. Tonton Garby is a sandwich perfectionist who tailor-makes each of his creations. Cheese is the star, supported by a tempting cast of fillings such as Belgian chorizo, papaya and honey.
6 Rue Duquesnoy, 1000

Brunch
Weekend feasts

①
Le Local, Louise
Brunch with a conscience

Founders Aubane Verger and Laura Perahia use ethical consumption as the building block for this elegant restaurant. The sourcing is impeccable, with much of the organic produce coming from nearby and fairtrade farms.

Le Local has as much style as substance, with geometric lampshades and a grooved pink wall. The Saturday brunch stretches over two or three courses, and includes all-you-can-eat breads and spreads. You'll be given a compostable bag filled with any leftovers.
51 Rue de la Longue Haie, 1000
+ 32 (0)2 647 6803
lelocalbxl.be

❷
La Petite Production, Flagey
All-week brunch

This little café ticks all the boxes on a brunch-spot wish list – and it does so, cheerily, every day of the week. The menu covers all bases, from healthy chia-seed breakfast bowls to hunger-busting cooked breakfasts with a choice of eggs. Nothing surprising, then, but little touches set it apart. Cloud-like pancakes come with a vial of extra syrup, fruity toppings vary with the cook's seasonal whims and the cold-pressed juice changes every day. Get here by 10.30, especially on the weekend, or be prepared to wait.
5 Rue du Couloir, 1050
lapetiteproduction.be

③
Les Filles, Dansaert
Hostess with the mostest

The three friends behind this canteen (which has two siblings, including one at Coudenberg Palace) have built their success on making diners feel at home. This iteration in an airy townhouse sets the mood with long communal tables, mismatched vintage crockery and an open kitchen.

Brunches are sociable buffet affairs, with pastries, farmhouse cheeses, eggs and fresh fruit, plus specials. A welcome change from the usual eggs Benedict and pancake stacks.
46 Rue du Vieux Marché aux Grains, 1000
+ 32 (0)2 534 0483
lesfilles.be

Coffee
Refuel

①
Belga & Co, Châtelain
Bean to cup

The sleek offspring of an Antwerp roastery, this coffee shop greets guests with the heady scent of quality beans. The interior is worldly and homely in equal measure: red-ochre walls, a bookshelf laden with novels and travel tomes, and an oversized African mask.

For owner Charly Meerbergen, a cup of coffee is all about the ritual, so sip yours with some degree of solemnity. Or take it into the leafy back garden, a sun trap with a long communal table and wooden benches.
7A Rue du Bailli, 1000
+ 32 (0)2 644 1498
belgacoffee.com

②
Mok Specialty Coffee Roastery & Bar, Dansaert
Wake-up call

Get your caffeine fix in this lab-like spot by the canal. One wall is lined with Porlex grinders, Aeropress filters and Moccamasters – all the kit you'd need to brew a serious cup at home. Thankfully, expert baristas do all the hard work here.

Coffee aficionados will appreciate printed tasting notes tracing the bean's journey from tropical smallholdings to Mok's micro-roastery in Leuven. Visit early to savour a precision brew in a hushed atmosphere and for all-day breakfasts (from cashew-cream toast to savoury porridge).
196 Rue Antoine Dansaert, 1000
+ 32 (0)495 316 718
mokcoffee.be

③
Moka, Dansaert
Caffeine hit

This petite venue pairs vintage good looks (original floor tiles, Formica tables and hanging plants aplenty) with a classic approach to coffee-making. You'll find no cold-brew kit here but rather a shiny Faema machine churning out perfect macchiatos, lungos and lattes from the house blend.

There's a solid selection of Dammann Frères teas, plus – this being Belgium – beer such as the artist-funded Illegaal. A short and sweet menu of breakfast bites, light lunches and home-baked cakes keeps hunger pangs at bay.
5 Rue des Riches Claires, 1000
+ 32 (0)473 767 345

Sweet treats
Beyond waffles

① Chouconut, Porte de Hal
Moreish morsels

For Baptiste Mandon and Ana Kebadze, this handsome tearoom is a labour of love. French pastry chef Mandon is the perfectionist behind the house's signature bite-sized choux and can happily spend two weeks tinkering with recipes for the next surprising flavour (strawberry and pistachio praline, at the time of writing). If, like Kebadze, you don't have much of a sweet tooth, opt for the zingy mango-passion fruit number instead of the best-selling salted caramel.
46 Avenue Jean Volders, 1060
+ 32 (0)2 537 1692
chouconut.com

② Coco Donuts, Châtelain
Hand-dipped delights

This light-filled doughnut shop may not be to everyone's taste – think neon wall art, an upstairs photo booth and a flower-crown-toting barista – but the brioche-dough rings are the real deal.

Dreamed up by friends Candice Tielemans and Chloé Sengier, these doughnuts are big (you may need a knife and fork) and boldly flavoured with the likes of violet or bacon and maple. The stream of people picking up pre-ordered boxes is a testament to its status as a neighbourhood fixture.
168 Chaussée de Charleroi, 1060
+ 32 (0)2 646 7155
cocodonutsbrussels.be

③ Gaston, Dansaert
Lickety-split

There's something deliciously retro about this ice-cream parlour's striped motif and red-capped gelato scoopers. It's at its best on sunny days, of course, when delighted customers drift across the Quai aux Briques to savour their cups and cones by the water – but the heated terrace is appealing year-round.

Everything is homemade from the very best ingredients (Valencia almonds, say, or Madagascan vanilla), with a few surprising flavour twists such as ginger, gin or Szechuan pepper. We'd be hard-pressed to pick a favourite, even after repeat visits, but the Iranian pistachio and Alphonso mango are definite frontrunners.
86 Quai aux Briques, 1000
+ 32 (0)2 223 4306
glaciergaston.be

Drinks
Santé!

① Le Citron Poilu, Louise
Tipples and tapas

This Mediterranean-inspired tapas bar (its name means "hairy lemon" in French) does *apéro* hour with gusto. Grab a seat at one of the handful of streetside tables or on the pleasant patio out the back for a pre-prandial drink. There's something for every thirst, from natural wines to beloved local beers.

An ever-changing *cicchetti* (small snacks) menu offers petite plates such as ceviche, burrata and pheasant meatballs to the peckish. Look out for the bar's sporadic but lively special events, which bring neighbours together over themed cocktails or a whole sliced-to-order ham.
118 Rue Lesbroussart, 1050
+ 32 (0)2 344 4232
citronpoilu.com

② La Pharmacie Anglaise, Quartier Royal
Steampunk cocktails

Cure whatever ails you in this meticulously recreated Victorian apothecary, housed in a neo-gothic building designed by famed Bruxellois architect Paul Saintenoy. Kitted out with taxidermy, jarred specimens and creeping foliage, this cocktail bar may have the air of an antiquated cabinet of curiosities but its experimental tipples are resolutely modern.

Bartenders use all the tricks of their trade – rare liqueurs, theatrical smoke and oversized garnishes – to create spectacular drinks worth their hefty price tag. Book ahead and settle in for the evening.
66 Coudenberg, 1000
+ 32 (0)489 560 736
lapharmacieanglaise.com

③ Monk, Dansaert
Fun worship

More inclined to hedonism than monastic restraint, this compact bar has bags of charm. It's a popular spot to sample Belgian beers: you'll find a rotating selection on tap, from a cherry-steeped Boon Kriek to sour, oak-matured Rodenbach.

The backroom buffet serves no-nonsense plates of spaghetti – just the thing if you're sticking around for one of the DJ sessions or live gigs. On the second and fourth Sundays of the month Lindy Hoppers push the grand piano to one side to take over the floor.
42 Rue Sainte-Catherine, 1000
+ 32 (0)2 511 7511
monk.be

Retail
—— Trading
places

Fashion
Top threads

Think of Brussels
and it's unlikely you'll
picture the city's in-
resident bureaucrats
wearing cutting-edge
clothing and shopping for
hand-thrown ceramics.
But don't be deceived:
Belgium's capital city
has increasingly become
a popular base for
Europe's creative set.

Due to its relative
affordability, booming
creative industry and
entrepreneurial spirit, as
well as its geographical
proximity to Paris, London
and Amsterdam, a new
generation of designers
has chosen to set up
shop here. Along with
Belgium's long-standing
design talent, these
new independent
retailers will take you
on a shopping spree
from central Dansaert
to the city's art nouveau
residential streets.

Ding ding
—
Maison Margiela's first
European boutique opened
in Dansaert in 2002. The
Paris-based luxury fashion
house was founded by the
enigmatic Belgian designer
Martin Margiela. Ring the bell to
explore the famous MM label.
maisonmargiela.com

①
Eva Velazquez, Brugmann-
Lepoutre
Custom treasures

Eva Velazquez established
her charming, eponymous
womenswear shop on Rue
Franz Merjay in 2015 with her
brother Hugo (*both pictured*).
The Barcelona natives cater to
anyone looking for long-lasting
pieces that are personal, ethical
and unique.

Eva sources fabrics from
flea markets and antique
shops on her travels around
the world and restores
Victorian blouses, dungarees
and military costumes into
feminine pieces. Hugo too
creates contemporary clothing
with equal attention to quality
and timeless materials. Defiant
of fast, disposable fashion, the
siblings' offering is entirely
designed and manufactured
in their Brussels workshop.
56 Rue Franz Merjay, 1050
+ 32 (0)2 223 0411
evavelazquez.be

②

Stijl, Dansaert
Style pioneer

Founded by Sonja Noël (*pictured*), Stijl has been instrumental in providing a platform for emerging and groundbreaking designers since it opened in 1984. Together with the Antwerp Six (*see pages 88 and 130*), Noël cleverly marketed Belgium as a cult fashion destination and the Rue Antoine Dansaert as its epicentre of high-end garms.

On sale are stalwart brands such as Dries Van Noten and Ann Demeulemeester, plus forward-thinking eco labels including Sofie d'Hoore and Jan-Jan Van Essche.

Womenswear: 74 Rue Antoine Dansaert, 1000
+32 (0)2 512 0313
Menswear: 6 Place du Nouveau Marché aux Grains, 1000
+32 (0)2 513 4250
stijl.be

③
Centreville, Dansaert
Ahead of the curve

This contemporary menswear shop has brought international streetwear to Brussels' fashion district since its inception in 2014. Located off Rue Antoine Dansaert, a street brimming with big-name Belgian designers, Centreville takes pride in discovering new brands, as well as predicting those due for a comeback.

Labels include New York's Aimé Leon Dore, Germany's A Kind of Guise, and Arte (*see page 86*). There's also an in-house T-shirt range. According to Nicolas Volckrick, who co-founded the business with Jérémy Baur (*both pictured, Baur on right*), the collection as a whole is "original, wearable, useful and technical".

36 Rue des Chartreux, 1000
+ 32 (0)2 513 5963
centrevillestore.com

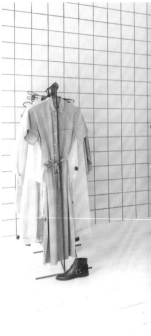

④
Reservoir Store, Louise
Scandinavian street style

Patrick De Wulf was looking for a spot away from the commercial shopping districts when he opened Reservoir Store near Place Eugène Flagey in 2009, spearheading a wave of independent retailers moving to the area. Since then he's merged his men's and womenswear branches: "We decided to group them because we work with brands where the difference between men's and women's collections are less clear," he says.

The multibrand shop focuses on quality clothing, bags and accessories from Scandinavian labels such as WoodWood and Our Legacy. Get your kicks around the corner at streetwear offshoot Reservoir 313.

43A Rue Lesbroussart, 1050
+ 32 (0)2 201 6002
reservoir-store.com

⑤
Bellerose, Hôtel des Monnaies
Elegant basics

This beloved Belgian brand
has shops across Europe. It
started in 1989 with a small
line of men's shirts inspired
by classic US workwear and
today its designs draw on
everything from Tokyo street
art to Indian retail logos.
Men and women will find
reliable staples, from basic
T-shirts to neat knitwear, while
collaborations with labels such
as French shoemaker Veja keep
things fresh.
    The team also takes
pride in its shop design: this
flagship store is housed in a
mansion and features plenty
of ornamental woodwork. The
Antwerp space is located in an
industrial former tram terminal.
5 Chaussée de Charleroi, 1060
+32 (0)2 539 4476
bellerose.be

⑥
Icon, Dansaert
Cutting-edge yet classic

The collection of womenswear
on offer at Icon features chic
items by both established
and emerging designers. The
racks bear everything from
timeless pieces by London
label Rejina Pyo to shoes
from By Far (based between
Bulgaria, Australia and
London) and printed silks
by Warsaw's Magda Butrym.
5 Place du Nouveau Marché
aux Grains, 1000
+32 (0)2 502 7151
icon-shop.be

Homeware
House proud

⑦
Uniform, Brugmann-Lepoutre
Strong designs

This smart menswear shop
stocks Italian brands known
for their high quality, from
Escuyer and Lardini to
Aspesi and La Fileria. "The
collections I like best are classic
and masculine," says founder
Alexandre Vermeersch.

Bolder Belgian labels also
have a home here: 7D provides
well-cut basics, plus there's
graphic knitwear by Christian
Wijnants. The clothes are
complemented by a handsome
selection of men's watches,
underwear, socks, scarves
and wallets.
58 Rue Franz Merjay, 1050
+ 32 (0)2 345 8818
uniform-menswear.com

①

Bautier, Bas Forest
Keeping it cosy

After 10 years working in the furniture industry as a freelance designer for international powerhouses Ligne Roset, Swedese, Stattmann Furniture and Idée, Marina Bautier (*pictured*) returned to her hometown and launched her brand in 2013. She offers a homely collection of oak beds, tables and desks – pieces that radiate simplicity and durability. There's also the in-house line of homeware, linen and ceramics designed to complement the furniture.

Bautier enjoys keeping things as local as possible: "My furniture is made a three-hour drive away in a family-owned carpentry workshop."
*314 Chaussée de Forest, 1190
+32 (0)2 520 0319
bautier.com*

②

Lulu, Brugmann-Lepoutre
Family affair

Founders and cousins Antoine and Mathieu Rentiers come from a long line of people passionate about homeware and furniture. "Our great-grandparents were cabinet-makers, our grandparents were furniture wholesalers and our parents were merchants," says Mathieu. "We named Lulu after our grandmother."

The duo found their dream location in a former garage and have retained its raw interior, adding a café for good measure. This huge space is filled with an almost overwhelming array of goods, from Scandinavian-style sideboards and dining sets to ceramics from Belgian design classic Serax.
*101 Rue du Page, 1050
+32 (0)2 537 2503
lulu-store.eu*

Books, records and stationery
Take note

①

Crevette Records, Marolles
Sound underground

Located in the lively Marolles neighbourhood, Crevette Records was founded in 2016 by Pim Thomas, a prominent figure in the Brussels music and nightlife scene. It attracts the city's best DJs, as well as vinyl enthusiasts looking to discover the latest in left-field electronic music – from experimental to disco and African.

Both new and second-hand records are available, in addition to high-quality rotary mixers, needles and headphones. Thomas also runs his own label that supports local acts and organises in-store DJ sessions. Head here to catch the sound of Brussels' underground nightlife by day.
*146 Rue Blaes, 1000
+32 (0)2 514 1146
crevetterecords.be*

Local favourite
—
Veals & Geeks – a vinyl shop on a cobbled street in the centre of town – is one for the collectors. It specialises in 1960s and 1970s psych and prog but you might also stumble across voodoo soul from New Orleans and Italian horror classics.
vealsandgeeks.com

Which way for retail therapy?

Le Typographe, Brugmann-Lepoutre
Press the issue

Belgium's historic print heartland may be Antwerp but Le Typographe is pressing ahead with a new take on the old trade. Behind the stationery-maker's shopfront in a narrow townhouse in Châtelain, its workshop produces tens of thousands of notebooks and cards a year using five heavy Heidelberg presses.

With its paper goods already stocked in some 700 shops around the world, Le Typographe has become an international affair. French founder Cédric Chauvelot learned his typographic skills at L'Institut Supérieur des Beaux Arts in Besançon.
67 Rue Americaine, 1050
+32 (0)2 345 1676
typographe.be

② Tipi Bookshop, Haut Saint-Gilles
DIY temple

When Andrea Copetti (*pictured*) spotted a gap in the Belgian media landscape for a bricks-and-mortar shop selling self-published photography books and magazines, he decided to fill it. The result was this charming affair.

Every surface is stacked with titles, either produced directly by artists or small independent publishers. Leafing through the piles may be time-consuming but, in our opinion, it's a fine way to spend an afternoon.
186 Rue de l'Hôtel des Monnaies, 1060
+32 (0)478 956 841
tipi-bookshop.be

Ⓐ

Peinture Fraîche, Châtelain
Print pilgrims

This firm favourite has been in business for 30 years. Owner Philippe Demoulin (*pictured, on right*) was a long-time customer before acquiring the bookshop in 2013. "Students are welcome, dogs are welcome, punks are welcome and there is no obligation to buy – you're even allowed to take a picture!" he says.

You'll discover many specialised books on art, architecture and design. And don't miss the gallery exhibiting work by local artists, photographers and designers.
10 Rue du Tabellion, 1050
+32 (0)2 537 1105
peinture-fraiche.be

Market special

The characterful flea market on the cobblestoned Place du Jeu de Balle has remained largely unchanged since its founding in 1873. It takes place 365 days a year in the formerly working-class Marolles neighbourhood.

To uncover a treasure you'll need to dig deep, not in your pockets but into the multitude of boxes and blankets at the chaotic market stalls. Haggling is half the fun and if you're lucky you'll be rewarded with a bargain. But more than anything, a trip here is about the experience.

This pocket of the city is authentically Brussels – so grab a seat at one of the outdoor tables of the old cafés and soak up the atmosphere. Tip: come on a weekday close to finish at 14.00 and you'll find cheap wares for a euro and full boxes of bric-a-brac up for grabs.
Place du Jeu de Balle, 1000
marcheauxpuces.be

Reading material and a handy perch. I know – inspired

Culture
—— State of
the art

Brussels' culture scene is evolving but what it's evolving into isn't quite clear. It isn't trying to be London or New York – it wouldn't want to be, with their steep prices. In fact, one of the things boosting Brussels' stature in the art world is its affordability: low rents have attracted a host of emerging artists and young gallerists.

The commercial-art scene is thriving, promoted by people-pulling fairs such as Art Brussels. Old guard including Almine Rech Gallery rub shoulders with new names championing all things offbeat. It's the same with big institutions: the Musées Royaux des Beaux-Arts de Belgique continue to attract the crowds in the historic city centre while, after a bit of a lull, contemporary curveballs are shaking things up further afield.

For a city dominated by politics, Brussels' nightlife is surprisingly pumping, and there are a number of arthouse cinemas to keep you content when the weather disappoints. While some big cities move to the same beat, the Belgian capital is happy dancing by itself – and with you, if you'll come and join it.

Museums and public galleries
The big hitters

①

Art & History Museum, Cinquantenaire
Treasure trove

Spanning antiquity to the 20th century, this diverse collection features everything from Egyptian death masks and European decorative arts to Peruvian textiles and Belgian carriages. In summer the Temple of Human Passions is open three afternoons a week; the neoclassical pavilion was built by the late Victor Horta (*see page 56*) in 1896 and plays host to sculptor Jef Lambeaux's marble bas-relief of writhing nudes engaged in both human pleasures and sins. The 19th-century plaster-cast workshop is a more straight-laced point of interest, with 4,000-plus moulds to peruse.
10 Parc du Cinquantenaire, 1000
+ 32 (0)2 741 7331
artandhistory.museum

Design destinations

01 **Mad, Dansaert:** A space promoting collaborations between business-owners and stylists, designers and other creatives. Exhibitions, seminars and fashion shows take place on the ground floor, while the upper levels are devoted to multipurpose workspaces.
mad.brussels

02 **Adam, Laeken:** It may be a bit of a schlep but the trip to Adam is worth the effort if 20th and 21st-century design is your thing. Its permanent exhibition of some 2,000 plastic objects – from everyday kitchen utensils to designer chairs – sprung from the personal collection of the artist Philippe Decelle.
adamuseum.be

03 **Eleven Steens, Haut Saint-Gilles:** Opened in 2019 under the artistic direction of Jean-Marc Dimanche, this gallery focuses on contemporary art, design, fashion, architecture and more. Budding curators work on exhibitions, which in turn shine a spotlight on emerging artists.
elevensteens.com

Rethinking history
———
After a five-year renovation, the Royal Museum for Central Africa reopened in 2019 as AfricaMuseum, with what it declared would be a "decolonised" vision. Whether or not it succeeded, it has fostered a much-needed debate about Belgium's past in the Congo.
africamuseum.be

❷
Mima, Molenbeek
Underground vision

Cultural entrepreneurs Michel and Florence de Launoit joined forces with Alice Van den Abeele and Raphaël Cruyt – the duo behind Alice Gallery (*see page 44*) – to found The Millennium Iconoclast Museum of Art (Mima) in 2016. It opened on the graffitied banks of the Bruxelles-Charleroi canal in up-and-coming Molenbeek with the aim to promote contemporary art and design.

The industrial space is home to a permanent collection of artwork created between 2000 and the present day, and temporary exhibitions and performances crop up throughout the year. The focus is wide-ranging and draws on various subcultures, from hip-hop and graphic design to skateboarding and urban art.
39-41 Quai du Hainaut, 1080
+ 32 (0)472 610 351
mimamuseum.eu

③

Wiels, Bas Forest
Creative brew

Housed in the former
Wielemans-Ceuppens brewery,
which was designed by Belgian
architect Adrien Blomme
in 1930, Wiels is worth a
visit for the architecture alone.
A rare example of a modernist
building in Brussels, the
imposing grey façade gives
way to a restored interior
that retains some of the
brewery's original equipment,
vast copper vats included.

Wiels doesn't have a
permanent collection; instead,
it presents rotating exhibitions
by both emerging and
established artists that reflect
the evolution of contemporary
art. The centre also hosts
international artists in residence
and has a comprehensive
education programme offering
workshops and seminars,
plus a well-stocked bookshop
and café.
354 Avenue Van Volxem, 1190
+ 32 (0)2 340 0053
wiels.org

This is our live art project, in case you were wondering

④
Musée Magritte, Quartier Royal
Iconic whimsy

Fluffy clouds, green apples and pipes: the signature imagery of René Magritte is ubiquitous and instantly recognisable. Perhaps the most important Belgian artist of the 20th century, he spent most of his life in Brussels. Where better, then, to view his art – witty works that surprise and delight.

Part of the Musées Royaux des Beaux-Arts de Belgique (we'd suggest buying a multi-pass ticket), this museum opened in the former Hôtel Altenloh in 2009. Over five floors it hosts the world's largest collection of the surrealist's works, from illustrations and engravings to paintings and photographs.
1 Koningsplein, 1000
+ 32 (0)2 508 3211
musee-magritte-museum.be

Commercial galleries
Arty business

①
Xavier Hufkens, Brugmann-Lepoutre
Artistic heavyweights

This prominent gallery, founded by Xavier Hufkens in 1987, has two permanent spaces in Brussels: a beautiful 19th-century townhouse at 6 Rue Saint-Georges (complete with garden) and, a few doors down, a new space designed by Swiss architect Harry Gugger in the mixed-use Rivoli galleries.

The focus is on contemporary art and a programme of hard-hitting solo exhibitions. It represents some 40 artists, from Daniel Buren to Tracey Emin, and partners with the estates of Robert Mapplethorpe, Louise Bourgeois, Willem de Kooning and Alice Neel.
6 & 107 Rue Saint-Georges, 1050
+ 32 (0)2 639 6730
xavierhufkens.com

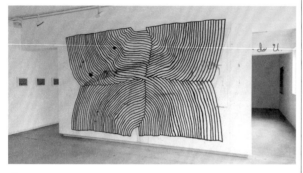

③

Galerie Greta Meert, Béguinage
Put in the picture

This Béguinage gallery is housed in a five-storey art nouveau building in downtown Brussels. Originally designed by Louis Bral, and renovated by Belgian architects Hilde Daem and Paul Robbrecht, the spacious structure is full of natural light thanks to its floor-to-ceiling windows.

Founding director Greta Meert opened the gallery under the name Galerie Meert Rihoux in 1988, with the first international exhibition of the young German photographer Thomas Struth. Today she and her son Frédéric Mariën continue to champion unknown talent and the gallery is hugely respected by both Belgian and international collectors. Minimal and conceptual art are the gallery's beat and photography is a particular interest.
13 Rue du Canal, 1000
+ 32 (0)2 219 1422
galeriegretameert.com

②
Alice Gallery, Dansaert
Up-and-comers

Alice Gallery was founded by Alice Van den Abeele and Raphaël Cruyt (*pictured*), two members of the quartet behind Mima (*see page 41*), down a quiet Dansaert alley in 2005. She has a degree in cultural management and has worked in galleries in London and New York, while he, among other things, has been a cartoonist and an IT entrepreneur.

The pair work with emerging artists and have a penchant for urban art, in which multiple artistic practices collide. There's also an exhibition space on the ground floor of the next-door building; on the upper storeys, the duo have three apartments available to rent (*see page 19*).
4 Rue du pays de Liège, 1000
+ 32 (0)2 513 3307
alicebxl.com

④

Maniera, Grand Place
Experimental design

Maniera invites artists and architects to extend beyond their usual practice and dabble in the world of product design. Founded in 2014 by Amaryllis Jacobs (*pictured*) and Kwinten Lavigne, the Grand Place gallery commissions limited-edition objects of use and pieces of furniture that blur the lines between creative practices.

As well as working with the next generation of makers, Jacobs and Lavigne collaborate with more established designers – such as Anne Holtrop and Jonathan Muecke – who have signature styles that can be channelled into highly original works. "We look for artists and architects who have a very specific design language," says Jacobs. "Nobody builds like Office Kersten Geers David Van Severen (known for its project Solo House) or Studio Mumbai, for instance. Their language is so clear you can almost pitch it in one line."
27-28 Place de la Justice, 1000
+32 (0)494 787 290
maniera.be

Galleries galore

01 **Clearing, Van Volxem-Van Haelen:** The Brussels outpost of this contemporary art gallery is located in a former shutter factory around the corner from Wiels (*see page 42*). It was founded in Brooklyn in 2011 and now represents almost 20 artists, as well as the estates of Bruno Gironcoli and Sir Eduardo Paolozzi. *c-l-e-a-r-i-n-g.com*

02 **Sorry We're Closed, Sablon:** Emerging and mid-career artists from Belgium and abroad are the order of the day at Sebastien Janssen's gallery on Rue de la Régance. Open from Wednesday to Saturday (as are many of Brussels' commercial galleries) with a combination of solo and group shows. *sorrywereclosed.com*

03 **Almine Rech, Brugmann-Lepoutre:** French collector and art dealer Almine Rech's eponymous gallery has outposts in London, Paris and New York. It has long-standing relationships with big-name artists such as James Turrell and represents Jeff Koons, Günther Förg and others. *alminerech.com*

04 **Atelier Jespers, Georges Henri:** The setting of this minimalist gallery – a modernist house by Belgian architect Victor Bourgeois (*see page 51*) – is as striking as the works within. Jean-François Declercq founded Atelier Jespers in 2015 and dedicated it to contemporary design. *atelierjespers.com*

②
Kanal-Centre Pompidou,
Quartier Maritime
Work in progress

Check the website before you
visit this canal-side complex,
which is sure to become a
major art destination but –
for the foreseeable future
– is undergoing a dramatic
overhaul. Before building
works began in 2019 there
were 14 months of exhibitions
in the former Citroën garage,
which provided a glimpse of
what's to come, and various
events will keep things ticking
over until its unveiling in 2023.

An offshoot of the Centre
Pompidou in Paris, Kanal
will be part modern and
contemporary museum – with
exhibitions that encompass
every discipline – and
part cultural centre, with a
wide range of events and
performances. It will also
feature major installations
by Belgian artists.
*Quai des Péniches, 1000
+ 32 (0)2 435 1360
kanal.brussels*

①
Palais des Beaux-Arts,
Quartier Royal
Widespread interests

The city's leading cultural
centre is housed in a vast
concrete-and-marble complex
on the Mont des Arts. The
largely subterranean art deco
compound was designed by
Victor Horta (*see page 56*).

The Palais des Beaux-Arts
(Bozar) has a cultural repertoire
to match its size, hosting major
international exhibitions,
literary events, dance and
theatre, and more than 300
concerts – classical music, jazz,
electronic and more – a year.
There's also a cinema screening
foreign films, a restaurant
headed by the Michelin-starred
chef Karen Torosyan and a
shop selling books on art,
architecture and design.
*23 Ravensteinstraat, 1000
+ 32 (0)2 507 8430
bozar.be*

Everybody dance now

01 Les Ateliers Claus,
Bosnie: A bastion for
independent music ever
since founder Frans Claus
began hosting concerts
in his home studio back
in the 1990s. Railing
against the cultural
standardisation of live
venues, his team's
commitment to the more
interesting acts out there
remains uncontested,
with the space acting
as a rallying point for the
city's experimental artists.
lesateliersclaus.com

02 Beursschouwburg,
Dansaert: This venue
distinguishes itself
through its laser-like
focus on the fringes: the
programme of lectures,
live concerts, screenings
and exhibitions makes
it one of the most
forward-thinking spots
in town. Check out the
popular rooftop sessions
in summer.
beursschouwburg.be

03 Flagey, Flagey: Boasting
some of the best
acoustics in Europe,
Flagey plays host to
different musical offerings
– from electronic, jazz
and classical festivals to
workshops and concerts
for kids. Be sure to check
out its Cinema section,
curated in collaboration
with Brussels' Cinematek.
flagey.be

04 C12, Quartier Royal:
Taking the local club
scene by storm, C12's
ability to book some
of the biggest acts to
grace the dance floor is
unmatched. Recent acts
have included Luke
Vibert, Orpheu the Wizard
and Kim Ann Foxman.
c12space.com

Cinemas
Silver screen

Palace, Dansaert
Grande dame

This independent cinema was
commissioned in 1913 by film
distributor Charles Pathé and
designed by Paul Hamesse. The
Pathé Palace was the biggest in
the city, with 2,500 seats, three
entrances and an elaborate
interior. Many renovations
later, it reopened in 2018 as
the equally striking Palace.

There are four screens
showing both mainstream
films and more offbeat shorts
and documentaries, all in their
original language with Dutch
and French subtitles. Belgian
films are also well represented.
85 Boulevard Anspach, 1000
+ 32 (0)2 503 5796
cinema-palace.be

②
Cinéma Galeries, Grand Place
Heritage hideout

When the rain begins to fall
make a beeline for this historic
cinema in the city centre.
Built in 1939 by the architect
Paul Bonduelle, the art deco
structure in the covered
Galeries Royales Saint-Hubert
was renovated in 1973 and is
now a listed monument.

It shows everything from the
latest releases to arthouse flicks
first presented at Europe's
leading film festivals and
retrospectives of celebrated
directors. The three screening
rooms regularly play films in
English (or with subtitles).
26 Galerie de la Reine, 1000
+ 32 (0)2 514 7498
galeries.be

Design and architecture
—— Built environment

Architecturally, Brussels is a city of extremes. On the one hand you'll find ornate – at times ostentatious – art nouveau townhouses; on the other, dystopian and exceedingly ambitious postmodern monsters. But there's much in between that many visitors neglect to see – or simply don't know about.

To start, the Belgian capital has swathes of world-class brutalist structures. Then there's the unique trove of modernist architecture by both homegrown talent – such as Victor Bourgeois – and first-rate architects from further afield. All are products of Belgium's faith in the future: grand structures in appropriately pioneering styles, whether that's the marble and stucco of art deco or the steel, glass and concrete of the 1960s.

Brussels has always been a forward-thinking city in that sense, and the outcome is a cityscape to gawp at. Whether in awe or horror is another question but one thing's for sure – Brussels is not one to inspire indifference.

①
Bâtiment Europa, Quartier Européen
Leading light

When the European Union outgrew the Justus Lipsius building, it needed a new headquarters. Designed by Belgian architect Sir Philippe Samyn, the Bâtiment Europa was completed in 2016 and incorporates the façade of a 1920s art deco apartment block by Michel Polak, thereby bridging old and new.

The wooden lattice exterior is made up of 3,750 recycled window frames and, inside, a bulbous glass structure containing conference rooms shines softly at night with low LEDS. The overall appearance is of a giant lantern, glowing amid the surrounding buildings. The only anomaly is the garish colour-block of room interiors by Belgian artist Georges Meurant. Open to the public once a year, on Europe Day in May.
175 Rue de la Loi, 1048
+ 32 (0)2 281 6111
consilium.europa.eu

❷
Herman Teirlinck Building, Quartier Maritime
Well balanced

The office building of the Flemish Government, completed in 2017 by Dutch practice Neutelings Riedijk Architects, is a quietly innovative blueprint for the city's architectural future. The six-storey span of its main block matches the height of the adjacent Tour & Taxis warehouses (*see page 57*), while its yellow-brick façade, divided into a Jenga-like pattern, evokes Belgian residential architecture.

It was built with recycled materials, uses geothermal energy for heating, and contains four internal gardens. Artists and poets decorated both the interior and exterior, injecting a dose of creativity.
88 Avenue du Port, 1000
+ 32 (0)2 553 1700
vlaanderen.be

Brutalist
Concrete creations

①
Bâtiment Marais, Martyrs
Urban drama

It's impossible to miss this building, whether or not you have an eye for architecture. The concrete, shark tooth-like façade stands out amid the drab postmodernism of the surrounding neighbourhood.

Architects Marcel Lambrichs, Casimir Grochowski & Daniel de Laveleye completed the experimental building for the Caisse Générale d'Épargne et de Retraite, a savings and pensions bank, in 1973. Today it belongs to BNP Paribas, and although this means no public access it does ensure the structure's longevity.
10 Rue des Boiteux, 1000

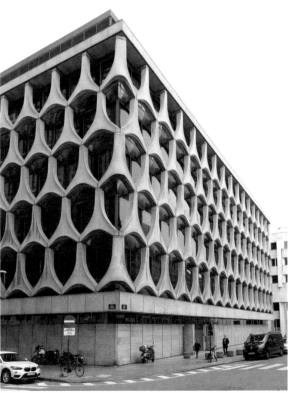

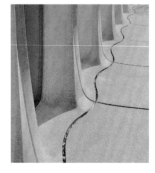

2

Fosbury & Sons Boitsfort,
Dries
Fabulous prefab

This building opened in 1970
as the HQ of Belgian concrete-
production firm CBR. Architect
Constantin Brodzki was
charged with showing the power
of the company's product.

It's a first-class example
of prefabricated architecture:
756 concrete modules, glass
included, that were assembled
on-site. Snaking channels
between each unit take care
of rainfall, meaning there's no
need for plastic piping, and
a heating system encased in
sapele wood veneer beautifully
lines the interior of each floor.

Today it's an office and
co-working space owned by
Fosbury & Sons, following a
sensitive renovation in 2018.
185 Chaussée de la Hulpe, 1170
+ 32 (0)2 793 1031
fosburyandsons.com/boitsfort

Modernist
Form and function

① Bâtiment Marnix, Quartier Européen
Quiet achiever

Completed in 1960 and currently belonging to ING Bank, this is US architect Gordon Bunshaft's only work in Belgium. Despite being party to the Brusselisation of the capital (*see page 13*), it has stood the test of time and secured a place in the pantheon of modernism. Primarily, this is thanks to the tasteful and complex execution of the prefabricated concrete façade, the many horizontal spines of which are held together by stainless-steel appendages. The effect is a uniform austerity that's rather fetching.
24 Avenue Marnix, 1000

All-seeing eye
──
The spectral Tour du Midi (South Tower) is a near-omnipresent sight in Brussels: it's always hovering above the cityscape no matter where you're looking. Though the building was completed in 1967, the severity and reflective glass exterior give it a postmodern feel.

② Atelier Jespers, Georges Henri
Art of the home

Belgian architect Victor Bourgeois built this home-cum-workshop for the sculptor Oscar Jespers (note the soaring ceiling for the artist's vast works). The curved windows, which let in ample sunlight, and the white façade are classic modernist tropes. It's now part-gallery (*see page 45*), part-home to art collector Jean-François Declercq, whose exhibitions range from late-modernist prints to giant contemporary sculptures – just as Jespers would have wanted.
149 Avenue du Prince Héritier, 1200
+32 (0)475 649 581
atelierjespers.com

③ Église Notre-Dame de Stockel, Stockel
Spirited design

Completed in 1967, the Église Notre-Dame de Stockel is perhaps the most distinctive of the city's modernist churches. Architects René Aerts and Paul Ramon worked simultaneously on the Tour du Midi (*see left*), and the glass-and-concrete façade is cut from similar cloth.

Inside, a natural light-filled upper chamber contrasts with a lower shrine animated by prismatic stained glass. The latter transitions from cold blue to almost pure sunlight as you get closer to the altar. A plan to top the building with an elaborate pyramidal tower was never realised, leaving the belfry exposed to the elements in a skeletal concrete frame.
82 Rue de l'Église, 1150
+32 (0)2 772 8737
ndstockel.be

Train stations
On the move

②

Bruxelles-Central, Quartier Royal
Journey's end

People are often surprised to learn that this station was designed by Victor Horta (*see page 56*), the don of art nouveau, but by 1910 he'd moved more towards the International style. Sadly, Horta never lived to see the project through: it was completed by his pupil Maxime Brunfaut in 1952.

Although Horta's restrained genius shines through, especially in the gently undulating exterior and curved ceiling lights, the station is dotted with tell-tales of the 1950s à la Bruxelles-Congrès (*see opposite*): in the main vestibule is an angular fresco by J Hayez of Saint Michael protecting Belgium, and to his right is a bas-relief depicting scenes of industry.
2 Carrefour de l'Europe, 1000

①

Bruxelles-Nord, Quartier Nord
Diamond in the rough

Brussels' northern station stands atop an older, 19th-century incarnation that was demolished to accommodate growing demand and bigger, faster trains. The long, slim structure with the imposing clock tower was designed in the 1930s by Paul Saintenoy and his son Jacques. Though Paul was an art nouveau man, the station is in the International style that took precedence in the late 1920s and early 1930s.

The tiered, dark-brown building to the west of the clock tower is a 1980s extension housing shops and offices. Unequivocally ugly, along with all the other postmodernist architecture in the area, the surroundings only serve to accentuate the main station's mid-century charm.
76 Rue du Progrès, 1030

③
Bruxelles-Congrès, Martyrs
What a relief

The early 20th century saw a big governmental push for a north-south rail link through Brussels. Along the route was Bruxelles-Congrès, designed by Maxime Brunfaut and completed in 1952; although rarely used nowadays, it's undoubtedly the most remarkable of the stations.

Brunfaut's functionalist building features a terracotta façade – it would have gleamed brightly back in the day – that contrasts neatly with the stone skeleton. Jozef Cantré's bas relief on the protruding tower depicts industry and human progress, while Robert Delnest's lateral relief channels the unity of Belgium and shows the country's major cities, surrounded once more by scenes of hard work.
25 Boulevard Pachéco, 1000

①
Palais des Expositions du
Heysel, Heysel
Anniversary present

The year 1935 marked the
centenary of the country's
founding, so to commemorate
the past and spur on the future
Brussels hosted a monumental
World Expo. The architecture
of the art deco main hall –
Palais des expositions du
Heysel, which is still an active
expo venue – reflects this
ambition, both in scale and
pioneering design.

Architect Joseph Van Neck's
pyramidal, concrete "palace"
has no interior support –
instead, the entire structure
is held on the strength of the
exterior. The front façade
features four pillars crowned
by four-metre-tall statues
showing forms of transport
from sailing to aviation.
On the ground are further
statues that pay homage to the
Belgian economy: agriculture,
commerce and so forth.
1 Place de Belgique, 1020

②

Villa Empain, Boondael
Past glory

This imposing villa blends art deco panache with Bauhaus sensibility. Architect Michel Polak designed it in 1932 for Louis, the son of industrialist Baron Édouard Empain, one of the world's richest men (so rich that he built a city, Heliopolis, from scratch near Cairo).

It fell into neglect in the mid-1990s but the Boghossians – a philanthropic family of Armenian jewellers who had fled from the genocide – restored the building in 2010 (sadly none of the furniture survived). As art deco is a marriage of western and eastern influences, it seems only right that art exhibitions by eastern artists are now held here.
67 Avenue Franklin Roosevelt, 1050
+ 32 (0)2 627 5230
villaempain.com

③

Palais Stoclet, Chant d'Oiseau
Career pinnacle

Commissioned by banker and art collector Adolphe Stoclet and completed in 1911, Palais Stoclet is the dizzying climax of Austrian architect Josef Hoffmann's genius. Strictly speaking the style is art nouveau but the angularity of the building suggests something that's evolving into art deco. Either way, one thing's for sure: this is a Gesamtkunstwerk, a "total work of art", and Hoffmann treated every little detail in the house as such.

The exterior is Carrara marble and bronze; inside, more marble, semi-precious stones and ornate furniture, not to mention a mosaic frieze by Gustav Klimt, the sketches for which are at the Museum Angewandte Kunst in Vienna. The Stoclet family still resides here, meaning it's sadly closed to the public, but there's plenty to gawp at from outside.
281 Avenue de Tervueren, 1150

Our house
—
Named after its architect Emile Hellemans, Cité Hellemans in Marolles is a very rare example of art nouveau social housing – indeed, one of the first examples of social housing at all. Though more than a century old, it's still inhabited today.
Rue des Tonneliers, 1000

Musée Horta, Châtelain
Art nouveau exemplar

Victor Horta's former house and workshop is a testament to his role as a pioneer of art nouveau. The movement sought inspiration from the natural world and was tied to the secular, socialist politics of the era; whereas, say, gothic architecture looked to the mysticism of God, art nouveau looked to the democratic, empirical beauty of nature.

This building, completed in 1901, is a treasure hunt of such symbolism: think brass door handles shaped like bulls' heads and lampshades resembling tulips. Horta also loved to mix materials, to singular effect: one wall might boast enamel bricks, wood, plaster and marble. To top it all off, he wired his home with advanced technology, including a pillar that doubles up as a radiator and a table with an in-built telephone – all of his own design, naturally.
25 Rue Américaine, 1060
+ 32 (0)2 543 0490
hortamuseum.be

We're very art nouveau, you know

① Palais de Justice, Marolles
Courting madness

Brooding above Brussels and capped with a bulging dome, the hulking neoclassical Palais de Justice cost the rough modern equivalent of €269m and took 17 years to complete, enveloping an entire neighbourhood in the process. Within is a series of titanic, Piranesi-esque hallways that defy conventional scale. Architect Joseph Poelaert died before the building work was finished in 1883 and rumours quickly spread that he'd been driven to madness by his megalomaniac project.

Though still a functioning court, many of the estimated 280 rooms remain unused. The Palais is in severe need of restoration: a longstanding Bruxellois joke holds that its protective scaffolding is itself scaffolded.
1 Place Poelaert, 1000
+ 32 (0)2 508 6111
justice.belgium.be

❷ Tour & Taxis, Quartier Maritime
Monumental metal

This vast former industrial site is replete with voluminous warehouses, plus a former train station. (The name is a French phonetic rendering of the German postal dynasty Thurn und Taxis, to whom parts of the land belonged.) Erected between 1902 and 1910, it fell into disrepair before being restored in the 2000s. It now houses shops, offices and one of Brussels' major exhibition venues.

The central structure, the Royal Depot, is a masterpiece of cast-iron engineering. Designed by Ernest Van Humbeeck, its huge neo-renaissance façade alternates between yellow brick and grey stone to form a startlingly ornamental whole. Inside, the glass-roofed main hall boasts four tiers of balconies crisscrossed by iron bridges.
86 C Avenue du Port, 1000
+ 32 (0)2 426 1222
tour-taxis.com

Residential
Our house

Enviable digs

At the dawn of the 20th century Belgium was a wealthy, industrious country. Brussels' well-to-do businessmen commissioned renowned architects – including Victor Horta, Gustave Strauven and Paul Hankar – to design for them lavish townhouses in affluent neighbourhoods such as Saint-Gilles. The result is eclectic but beautiful – a mix of art nouveau, art deco, Byzantine-inspired and Palladian-esque styles. Some streets are veritable museums without a modern structure in sight.

They may be hotly valued and much sought after now but after the Second World War Brussels had lost interest in historic architecture, and beautiful homes were torn down to make way for glass, steel and concrete. Progress is all well and good but Belgium put too much faith in the promise of modernity. Construction was unbridled and the architecture often poor, which explains why the city centre is in an uncomely state now.

Thankfully the suburbs have been largely untouched by Brusselisation – as the postwar building period is known – and, as such, there are still plenty of houses to admire.

Café culture

For a more intimate encounter with art nouveau, pop into Taverne Greenwich for a coffee or lunch. Completed in 1916, it has recently undergone a meticulous restoration. Oh, and Renée Magritte used to hang out there in his heyday. *greenwich-cafe.be*

Sport and fitness
—— Winning moves

Brussels is not a city known for its love of healthful pursuits but that doesn't mean there aren't options for those seeking to work off all those frites. When the weather is inclement we recommend heading indoors for a spot of climbing or a couple of laps; clear days call for some tennis or a few rings around one of the city's leafy parks. Happily, with the green spaces on our list offering eagle-eye vistas alongside grand architecture, lacing up doubles as sightseeing.

(1)
Petite Île, Industrie Sud
On the up

Brussels' first indoor centre for bouldering opened its doors in 2018 in a former factory. It offers about 100 different climbing routes, encompassing a wide range of grades. The in-house bar has an impressive beer list and a menu of vegetable-based dishes, making it a good spot to unwind after an intense scramble on the walls.
1A Rue de la Petite Île, 1070
+ 32 (0)491 951 248
petite-ile.be

(2)
Piscine Victor Boin, Bosnie
Master stroke

Ringed by dressing rooms, this historic swimming pool was inaugurated in 1905 and completely remodelled in art deco style in the late 1930s. In 1974 it was renamed after Belgian swimmer Victor Boin.
    The pool can get crowded with school groups during the day so it's best visited early in the morning or in the late afternoon. Bear in mind that professional swimwear (read: speedos) and swim caps are required – those in beachwear will be turned away.
38 Rue de la Perche, 1060
+ 32 (0)2 539 0615
stgilles.brussels/places/la-piscine-communale-victor-boin

Displacement theory be damned!

Parks
Outdoor pursuits

① Parc Josaphat, Schaerbeek
Green haven

This park in the northeast of the city is a popular jogging spot. Its hilly landscape can be a little challenging but the early 20th-century landscaping is a just reward for your efforts. Highlights are a 500-metre-long trail following a creek and the wide road around the central lawn.

For those with extra energy, a fitness circuit of exercise stations can be found throughout the park. There's also a miniature-golf club, in the shadow of the Residence Brusilia, and an archery club that offers workshops for casual punters.
Parc Josaphat, 1030

② Parc Duden and Parc de Forest
Double act

These two picturesque spaces connect the lively municipalities of Saint-Gilles and Forest. With an elevation gain of 100 metres, the jogging route on offer is not for the faint of heart – but in return you'll get to enjoy stunning views. The highest segment – in Parc Duden around the Luca School of Arts – is particularly scenic at night when the city is lit up. If you're in the mood for some intense muscle training, hit the stairs between the two parks.
Parc Duden, 1190
Parc de Forest, 1190

Lawn and order
—
Fancy knocking a ball about? Tennis Club de Belgique, built in 1954, is as central as it gets. The three covered courts are often reserved for members but it's always worth popping in to check availability.
tennisclubdebelgique.be

③ Parc de Bruxelles, Quartier Royal
Dignified activity

This rectangular park in the heart of the capital is between the prime minister's office at 16 Rue de la Loi and the Palais Royal de Bruxelles. Designed to facilitate an effortless crossing on foot for dignitaries, the park is the setting for a variety of runs: short lunch-break jogs, intense interval sprints or multiple laps of the 1.4km outer track. We recommend you enjoy the music of online station Kiosk Radio while you run, which streams from a wooden shack at the centre of the park also offering refreshments.
Place des Palais, 1000

Walk
—— Pound the pavement

When you arrive in Brussels, the city may not feel fit for an afternoon promenade or a midnight stroll – but that's probably because you've disembarked in the dense centre. Further afield in neighbourhoods such as Quartier Européen, Chasse and Porte de Hal you'll find quaint, tree-lined streets filled with cafés, pretty shops and grand townhouses. For this guide, we've picked two of our favourites patches to explore on foot.

Saint-Gilles and Châtelain
Suburban lights

Strangely enough, real Brussels is to be found in the suburbs. Neighbourhoods such as Saint-Gilles and Châtelain, where this walk takes you, developed into wealthy enclaves at the turn of the past century and have been spared the unbridled, and unattractive, postwar building boom that blighted the city centre. Accordingly, they boast immaculate streets lined with art nouveau and art deco townhouses. Over the years these suburbs have become little epicentres in their own right, displaying an alternative side to the Belgian capital, with fine restaurants, wine bars and retail treasures aplenty. *Suivez-nous!*

Architecture, bars and buys
Saint-Gilles and Châtelain walk

Start by fuelling up at patisserie
1 *Ginkgo*, which arguably makes the best pecan pain au chocolat that our reporters have ever tasted (for something lighter, we recommend the airy Paris-Brest pastry).

Exit, cross the square and walk west along Rue Jourdan; take the second right and then left onto Rue de la Filature, continuing straight until it becomes **2** *Rue Vanderschrick*. This stretch of road boasts impeccably preserved art nouveau townhouses; it's rare to find so many side by side.

At the far end of the road, turn left onto Rue Dethy and head east. Turn left at the end and then immediately right onto Rue Louis Coenen. Continue straight for three blocks, admiring the storied residential architecture. A right turn down Place Louis

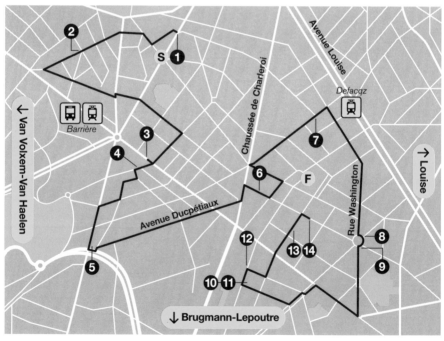

Morichar and another two blocks brings you to ❸ *Café La Pompe*, in the heart of Saint-Gilles. This spot is an all-rounder, offering coffee, drinks and lunch alike.

A few doors down is ❹ *Art Déco Antiquités*, which, as the name attests, specialises in furniture, art and home decor from the art deco period. Around the corner on Place Maurice Van Meenen is Hôtel de Ville de Saint-Gilles, an imposing neighbourhood government office (open to the public).

Walk around the Hôtel, turn right on Rue de Savoie, then shoot south on Chaussée d'Alsemberg until you reach ❺ *Bar du Matin*. This is a lively neighbourhood gathering spot. Grab a *pintje* (small beer) or make a note to come back later.

Head east along Avenue Ducéptieux – past a rather absurd 19th-century, still-functioning prison – until you

hit Chaussée de Charleroi, which marks the boundary between Saint-Gilles and Châtelain. Veer left then right at Rue Américaine and you'll come to ❻ *Musée Horta*, the former home and workshop of art nouveau pioneer Victor Horta (*see page 56*).

Like Saint-Gilles, this *quartier* boasts some of the finest early-20th century architecture in Brussels. Head north on Rue Africaine, left

onto Rue de l'Aqueduc, then follow Rue Defacqz to the ornate ❼ *Maison Ciamberlani*. Built in 1897 by architect Paul Hankar – who also built number 71 – it features an allegorical sgraffito façade.

Now for a little retail therapy. Facing the house, walk left and then turn right down Rue de Livourne. Continue straight and you'll soon reach Henri Michaux Square. On the north side is ❽ *Thibaut Wolvesperges Art & Furniture*, touting 1950s, 1960s and 1970s design. To the south is bag-maker and leather goods specialist ❾ *La Maroquinerie*.

Exit left then take the first right to walk along Chaussée de Waterloo. Another left onto Avenue Louis Lepoutre, followed by a right down Rue Emmanuel Van Driessche, brings you to menswear multibrand ❿ *Uniform* (*see page 36*), which stocks the likes of Aspesi. Next door is womenswear designer ⓫ *Eva Velázquez* (*see page 32*).

If you fancy an aperitivo, pop into cheery bar ⓬ *Chez Franz*, just up the road. Then a short stroll back into the centre of Châtelain via Rue Fernand Neuray (one block east) brings you to ⓭ *L'Épicerie – Cuisine du Marché* for a casual homemade lunch or ⓮ *Le Bout de Gras* (*see page 20*), which has an excellent wine selection, for something more hearty after all that walking.

Address book

01 Ginkgo
8 Place Julien Dillens, 1060
+32 (0)2 361 0929
ginkgopatisserie.be

02 Rue Vanderschrick
Rue Vanderschrick, 1060

03 Café La Pompe
211 Chaussée de
Waterloo, 1060
+32 (0)470 425 100
cafelapompe.be

04 Art Déco Antiquités
16 Avenue Adolphe
Demeur, 1060
+32 (0)2 534 7025
artdecoannebastin.be

05 Bar du Matin
172 Chaussée
d'Alsemberg, 1190
+32 (0)2 537 7159
bardumatin.be

06 Musée Horta
25 Rue Américaine, 1060
+32 (0)2 543 0490
hortamuseum.be

07 Maison Ciamberlani
48 Rue Defacqz, 1050

08 Thibaut Wolvesperges
Art & Furniture
154 Rue Washington,
1050
+32 (0)477 350 081
wolvesperges.com

09 La Maroquinerie
174 Rue Washington, 1050
+32 (0)2 344 7808
lamaroquinerie-bruxelles.be

10 Uniform
58 Rue Franz Merjay, 1050
+32 (0)2 345 8818
uniform-menswear.com

11 Eva Velazquez
56 Rue Franz Merjay, 1050
+32 (0)2 223 0411
evavelazquez.be

12 Chez Franz
30 Avenue du Haut-Pont,
1050
+32 (0)2 347 4212
chezfranz.com

13 L'Épicerie – Cuisine du
Marché
66 Rue du Page, 1050
+32 (0)477 986 029

14 Le Bout de Gras
89 Rue Américaine, 1050
+32 (0)488 160 012
leboutdegras.be

Antwerp

*Did someone say diamonds? I'll be your guide
to all of Antwerp's gems!*

Welcome
—— Announcing
Antwerp

We've taken a shine to a lot more than the famous *diamonds* in Belgium's second city; it's a gleaming centre for business, design and fashion too. Nestled between the North Sea and Belgium's bucolic Flanders region, and clustered around the *Schelde* river, it's best explored by bicycle and offers a picturesque mix of cobbled lanes and gothic, baroque and contemporary architecture.

Antwerp has long been a *vibrant port* and *trading hub*: it has been an entry point to continental Europe since the Middle Ages. This position ushered in a golden age of *art and culture* (the city is the home turf of baroque artist Peter Paul Rubens and his star apprentice Anthony Van Dyck, after all). Later, naval trade transformed the city into a *commercial centre* through which millions of travellers passed annually.

Today its strength is its *eye for design*. The emergence of a handful of forward-thinking fashion designers (*the "Antwerp Six"*) put the city on the map in the early 1980s and offered a glimpse of its potential in the creative industries. *Dries Van Noten* continues to reign but young entrepreneurs are causing a stir too. And on a larger scale, big-name architects from both Flanders and further afield are shaking up the cityscape with sparkling new structures.

Antwerp's walkable nature, postcard-pretty streets and independent shops make for *small-town charm* with *worldly appeal*. Read on for our round-up of what not to miss on a visit to this Flemish gem. — (M)

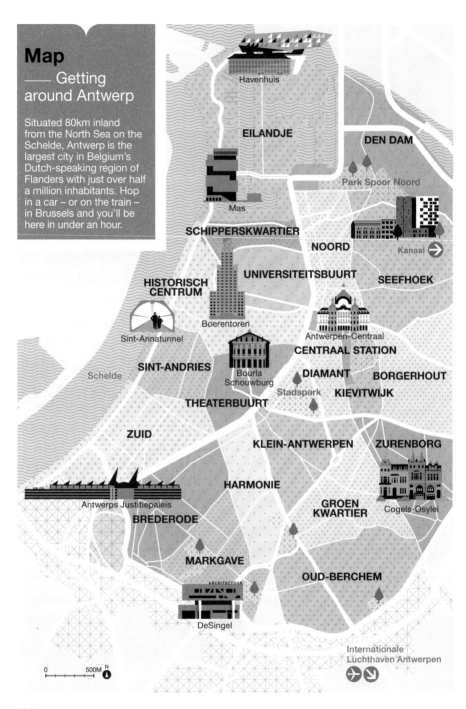

Map
—— Getting around Antwerp

Situated 80km inland from the North Sea on the Schelde, Antwerp is the largest city in Belgium's Dutch-speaking region of Flanders with just over half a million inhabitants. Hop in a car – or on the train – in Brussels and you'll be here in under an hour.

Havenhuis

EILANDJE

DEN DAM

Park Spoor Noord

Mas

SCHIPPERSKWARTIER

NOORD

Kanaal

UNIVERSITEITSBUURT

SEEFHOEK

HISTORISCH CENTRUM

Boerentoren

Sint-Annatunnel

Antwerpen-Centraal

CENTRAAL STATION

Schelde

SINT-ANDRIES

Bourla Schouwburg

DIAMANT

BORGERHOUT

Stadspark

KIEVITWIJK

THEATERBUURT

ZUID

KLEIN-ANTWERPEN

ZURENBORG

Antwerps Justitiepaleis

HARMONIE

GROEN KWARTIER

Cogels-Osylei

BREDERODE

MARKGAVE

OUD-BERCHEM

ARCHITECTUUR

DeSingel

Internationale Luchthaven Antwerpen

0   500M   N

Need to know
—— Get to grips with the basics

Cycling
On your bike

Antwerp is moving fast when it comes to cementing a cycling culture within the city and in 2011 a decent bike-sharing scheme arrived, called Velo Antwerpen. There are more than 4,000 bright-red bikes available from some 300 Velo stations, with more to be added in due course. Rent one by signing up online – a week costs €10; you'll be given a user number and pin, which you plug into any bike station screen and off you go. Just be careful when cycling along the tram tracks, lest your wheels get caught in the gaps.

The port
Water baby

Antwerp's history is tied to the sea. It's the largest port in Belgium and second only to Rotterdam in Europe. It's also Europe's biggest centre for the production and distribution of chemical and petrochemical products. Ships have docked here since medieval times and today it's linked to 800 ports around the world. The historic harbour handles 235 million tonnes of goods a year.

Diamonds
Take a shine

Antwerp has been a hub of the global diamond trade for centuries and today some 80 per cent of the world's rough diamonds pass through the city. There are about 4,500 traders, some Armenian, others Russian and Indian, but most Jewish and living in the vicinity of the appropriately named neighbourhood Diamant.

The link between diamonds and Antwerp has several roots; in part it dates back to 1476, when a man called Lodewyk Van Bercken invented the scaif, a polishing tool that used olive oil and diamond dust to give diamonds their pristine, multi-faceted appearance. The new technology put Antwerp ahead of other diamond-trading cities and laid the groundwork for its prestige.

Fashion
Dress to impress

Antwerp's Royal Academy of Fine Arts, whose fashion department is world-famous, has produced scores of talents, among them the Antwerp Six (see pages 88 and 130). The talented group – including Dries Van Noten and Ann Demeulemeester (see pages 86 and 88) – graduated in 1981 and showed their creations at the British Designer Show five years later. Suddenly, everyone was talking about Belgium. The Six set the tone for the country's fashion scene, with Antwerp as its mecca, and spurred on numerous other designers. Which explains why the city's retail scene is so buzzy.

Our top picks:

01 **Hotel Pilar:** Seventeen vast rooms plus a bustling restaurant and bar.
see pages 68-69

02 **Barchel:** Brunch in an elegant spot metres from Stadspark.
see page 81

03 **Graanmarkt 13:** Sleep, shop, eat, repeat.
see pages 70, 80 and 90

04 **Mas:** Antwerp's municipal museum is a wonder inside and out.
see pages 98 and 106

05 **Native:** Vegetarians and vegans will delight in this intimate, calm café.
see page 80

06 **Middelheimmuseum:** A picturesque alfresco art and sculpture museum featuring Ai Weiwei, Henry Moore and, well, more.
see page 97

07 **Sint-Annatunnel:** Take this 20th-century passage beneath the Schelde.
see page 108

08 **Le John:** A menu with Mediterranean flavours.
see page 78

09 **Boekenberg Swimming Pond:** This open-air complex is free to visit.
see page 114

10 **DeSingel:** Dance, theatre and music in a modernist building by Léon Stynen.
see page 101

Race you through the Sint-Annatunnel!

Hotels
—— Turn in

Antwerp has long had a crop of plush hotels, what with the port and diamond trade attracting well-heeled visitors in droves. But the past few years have seen a renaissance in the city's hospitality industry, as independent hoteliers have teamed up with top architects to create unique and elegant places to stay. Here we've nominated our pick of the bunch, from a grand affair in a former military hospital to a 19th-century manor turned five-room guesthouse.

①
Hotel Pilar, Zuid
Welcome respite

Many of Antwerp's upscale hotels hide behind walls of exclusivity: buzzers to get in; haughty concierges. Not so at Hotel Pilar. "We wanted to position ourselves between a Paris and Berlin-style hotel," says owner Christophe Ysewyn (*pictured, on right*) – that is, elegant hospitality and a democratic cool.

The heart of the operation is the ground-floor restaurant and bar, which is bustling from breakfast til nightcap and offers an eclectic menu riffing on Mediterranean and Middle Eastern cuisine. Upstairs are 17 enormous rooms, each of which has a king-size bed plus bath and shower. The interiors were handled by Ysewyn's husband Sam Peeters (*pictured, on left*), a designer who runs his own agency, Contekst.
34 Leopold de Waelplaats, 2000
+32 (0)3 292 6510
hotelpilar.be

MONOCLE COMMENT: The homeware shop adjoining the restaurant is stocked with abstract art, Pilar's own line of ceramics, furniture collaborations and more.

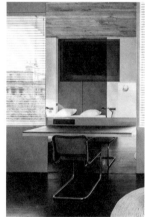

2

August, Groen Kwartier
Convenient find

When Belgian hotelier Mouche
Van Hool visited a 120-year-
old Augustinian convent in
Antwerp five years ago, she
knew it had potential. Together
with Callebaut Architecten
– a specialist in cultural and
historical projects – and Vincent
Van Duysen Architects, she
brought the building back to
life, restoring the original tiles,
brick walls and bubble-glass
windows and combining them
with modern details such as a
concrete-and-steel entrance.
5 Jules Bordetstraat, 2018
+32 (0)3 500 8080
august-antwerp.com

MONOCLE COMMENT: Though
each has Molteni&C furniture,
all 44 rooms and suites are
different. The former nuns'
quarters are petite while others
are more spacious.

Group stay
──
Graanmarkt 13 (*see pages
80 and 90*) offers a luxury
apartment that boasts four
bedrooms and an open-plan
living space. The aesthetic is
minimalist, in keeping with the
shop and restaurant downstairs.
A sound option for groups
after some privacy.
graanmarkt13.com

ALLES voor de REIS · RIGA · KOFFERS voor AFRIKA

(3)
Hotel Riga, Historisch Centrum
Just our type

Behind the front desk at Hotel Riga in the old town you'll find a battered wooden shutter that belonged to the building's former occupier and namesake, Marcel Riga, a purveyor of travel trunks. Though the structure had to be gutted to make way for this hotel, which opened in 2018, other vestiges of history are on show throughout: flagstone floors here, a timber beam there.

All 12 rooms are generously sized and three of the premier chambers occupy a separate 16th-century building that was once a paint shop frequented by Vincent Van Gogh. Small touches reveal the hotel's dedication to detail, including a bespoke font. "The difference between good and excellent is in the details," says owner Olivier Reyniers.
4 Korte Koepoortstraat, 2000
+ 32 (0)3 369 4422
hotelriga.be

MONOCLE COMMENT: The in-house Italian restaurant serves breakfast, lunch and dinner. For something more decadent, nip next door to Riga's fine-dining venue In de Balans (*see page 76*).

④

Hotel Julien, Historisch
Centrum
Well-appointed boutique

This 21-key hotel opened in
2004 and was the first venture
by Mouche Van Hool, who
also owns August (*see page 70*).
She's behind the decor here and
could well have made a living
as a designer – Hotel Julien
is whitewashed minimalism,
marble counters and small
touches of colour, all juxtaposed
against the 16th-century
building's historic trimmings.

The rooms, which make
the most of the daylight, are
decadently spacious and
decked out with furniture
by the likes of Vitra and
Eames, plus art on loan from
Antwerp's Gallery Fifty One
(pieces from the latter are
available to purchase). Two
of the rooms even have private
terraces. But the best part is
upstairs: the rooftop has views
of the cathedral and is the envy
of Antwerp on a summer's day.
24 Korte Nieuwstraat, 2000
+ 32 (0)3 229 0600
hotel-julien.com

MONOCLE COMMENT: The bar
serves Ottolenghi-style cuisine
all day, perfect for a late meal
after a night on the tiles.

(5)
Boulevard Leopold,
Groen Kwartier
Singular stay

With all the stately townhouses in Antwerp, it's no surprise that some have been converted into guesthouses. One such example is Boulevard Leopold on the edge of the Jewish quarter. Built in the 1890s, it features three large rooms and two suites. The flooring is original parquet and ceilings are high enough for a game of volleyball (though best not test that theory).

Owner Martin Willems bought the venture from his friends in 2010: he had helped out every now and then and found it to his liking. Willems' predilection for interior design lined him up perfectly for the role. The look is perhaps best described as Victorian adventurer meets antiquarian and makes for an inimitable backdrop to a stay.
135 Belgiëlei, 2018
+32 (0)486 675 838
boulevard-leopold.be

MONOCLE COMMENT: After a hearty breakfast, guests are invited to relax in Willems' private living room – though in the summer they often opt for the wisteria-laden courtyard.

Food and drink
—— Flemish fare

Once upon a time Flemish food meant little more than hearty farmers' fodder. And while that certainly still has a place – cue time-tested classics such as *stoofvlees* (beef stew) – Antwerp's food scene has been revolutionised of late.

Today the Michelin star-strewn port city rewards those with a taste for fine dining while also harbouring a new generation of iconoclastic chefs: the kind apt to source produce from a rooftop beehive or upend the typical Belgian focus on meat.

That same spirit of adventure animates all levels of the food chain, all the way up from the eclectic street-food joints offering fishy fast food or reinventing the humble frite. What's more, no matter the establishment, impressive design credentials are a constant.

We've also tapped the city's fine armada of bakeries and got to grips with its vibrant drinking culture. From timeworn brown bars to hip cocktail joints, in Antwerp everything goes – even a Unesco-listed cathedral serving beer.

①
The Jane, Groen Kwartier
Culinary worship

Food is religion in the chapel of this former military hospital, which chef Nick Bril (*pictured*) and his mentor Sergio Herman turned into a Michelin-starred restaurant in 2014. Today it's Antwerp's most oversubscribed dinner spot and a showcase for the duo's "rock'n'roll fine dining" approach.

You'll need to reserve three months ahead and make a pilgrimage to out-of-the-way Groen Kwartier, but Bril's tasting menus – which offer globetrotting combinations such as truffle and foie gras plus edible flowers – more than compensate. The art isn't just on the plate either, with Dutch designer Piet Boon's decor starring wonderfully kitsch contemporary stained-glass windows. If it's full, try the more accessible Upper Room Bar, which adds izakaya-style Asian tapas to the mix.
1 Paradeplein, 2018
+ 32 (0)3 808 4465
thejaneantwerp.com

I have a tendency to waffle on a bit

②
Fiskebar, Zuid
Sea and be seen

Make the most of this fish restaurant on Marnixplaats, Zuid's most appealing drinking hub, by kicking off with an aperitif at one of the square's many bars. The buzzing, youthful vibe continues inside this Scandi-style hangout, which has long played host to some of the finest seafood in town.

Co-owner Nikolaj Kovdal uses catch from European waters and sources vegetables from a nearby organic farm, with the house stars being bouillabaisse and semi-baked organic salmon. Pop in on a weekday for a good-value fish lunch; and check out the new and more casual Eilandje offshoot, Fiskeskur.
11 Marnixplaats, 2000
+ 32 (0)3 257 1357
fiskebar.be

③
In de Balans, Historisch
Centrum
Fine pedigree

The late-gothic letters on the
sign reveal a rich history: from
1848 until 2013 this site housed
Antwerp's oldest shop. "It was
a specialist store where Van
Gogh used to buy paint," says
Olivier Reyniers, who bought
the building in 2017.

Apparently the odd punter
still pops by for paint only
to find a temple to Belgian-
French gastronomy, albeit with
the chef's Italian background
often shining through. "Most
restaurants specialise but we
serve an equal number of fish,
meat and vegetarian dishes,"
says Reyniers. "We try to keep
a balance, like our name." His
family also runs the next-door
Hotel Riga (*see page 71*).
7 Kaasrui, 2000
+ 32 (0)3 226 3175
indebalans.be

Must-try
Stoofvlees from De Arme
Duivel, Theaterbuurt
On a winter's day, a generous
serving of *stoofvlees* (beef
stew) raises the spirits. There
are infinite variations but the
basic recipe involves slow-
cooked beef with onions,
brown or red ale, herbs,
vinegar and mustard. The
version offered by chef Nick
Van Linden at this brown café
has long been hailed as the
city's best; he uses wholegrain
mustard and adds madras
curry to his stock.
armeduivel.be

④
Dôme Sur Mer, Zurenborg
Prime catch

An aquarium wall advertises
the lure of Frédéric Chabbert's
sleek sibling to the Michelin-
starred Dôme across the street.
Come for irreproachably fresh
seafood a la plancha, best
abetted by oysters and a
crisp Pouilly-Fumé.

In summer there are few
finer places to graze than the
lovely terrace, tucked away in
the city's most architecturally
blessed neighbourhood (*see
pages 109 and 116*). If the
weather isn't on your side,
plump for the bar to admire
the chefs at work. And do leave
room for carbohydrates: the
complimentary bread comes
courtesy of the beloved next-
door bakery, Domestic (*see page
83*), and is the best of the best.
1 Arendstraat, 2018
+ 32 (0)3 281 7433
domesurmer.be

⑥ Bistrot du Nord, Noord
Northern star

Denizens of outlying Antwerp North were overjoyed at the 2013 opening of this art deco bistro, now the holder of a Michelin star, that combines the pleasures of a welcoming neighbourhood restaurant with flawless classical cooking.

Buzz the doorbell and you'll be spirited *à table* by co-owner Caroline Stasseyns, whose husband Michaël Rewers – a former chef at esteemed haunts Sir Anthony Van Dijck and 't Fornuis – parlays simple ingredients into unfussy yet creative dishes. Among the surprising amuse-bouches and satisfying meat and fish mains, carnivores are particularly well catered for thanks to Rewers' penchant for offal.
36 Lange Dijkstraat, 2060
+ 32 (0)3 233 4549
bistrotdunord.be

⑤ Ciro's, Zuid
Old-school rules

Opened in 1962 by Albert De Herdt, a former footballer for Belgium, this fuss-free brasserie is a classy spot with one foot in the past. The time warp begins with the candy-striped awning and continues into the wood-panelled interior.

The smartly dressed staff, animated atmosphere and unrepentantly carnivorous menu attract a loyal clientele of international business folk hungry for the daily special: the legendary Steak Ciro's, a classic since day one, served with hand-cut frites and six sauces on a wooden palette. For dessert, the *café glacé* (coffee ice cream) is elevated by its presentation in an old-fashioned silver coupe.
6 Amerikalei, 2000
+ 32 (0)3 238 1147
ciros.be

⑦ Table Dance, Historisch Centrum
Poles apart

This artfully sparse venture feels far too sophisticated for its setting – though a sly wink is given in the striptease pole bisecting the communal table.

Set up by young couple Michelle Woods, a former pastry chef at London's esteemed St John, and Roman Hiele, it offers relaxed, seasonal small plates – many informed by Woods' Filipino roots (the souped-up butter mochi is a joy). Stay for the parties with international DJs and acoustic acts.
25 Sint-Paulusplaats, 2000
+ 32 (0)483 474 070
tabledance.be

⑧
Veranda, Den Dam
Sui generis

This industrial-chic venue displays a sign warding off the Michelin men, who are not of interest to unconventional chef Davy Schellemans (*pictured*). All others, however, are welcome to walk in and enjoy his stellar five-course dinners.

"I love vegetables so I always start with those," says Schellemans. If he's satisfied with a dish it can stay on the menu for three weeks, otherwise it might change six days in a row. "Our sommelier hates it!" he adds. "There are no rules."
34 Lange Lobroekstraat, 2060
+32 (0)3 218 5595
restaurantveranda.be

⑨
Le John, Theaterbuurt
Too cool for school

Concealed behind the façade of an art deco secondary school, this staple of the Antwerp creative set is elevated by its strikingly sober mid-century decor: all muted browns and (aptly) Friso Kramer Revolt chairs, often used in classrooms.

The regularly changing, succinct menu veers towards Mediterranean flavours, with especially satisfying pasta and meat dishes. No need to move on for a nightcap: the low-lit upstairs bar is as intimate as a private home, at least one with an impeccable array of malt whiskies. And, as in a private home, you can also smoke, which may or may not be a positive.
25 Kasteelpleinstraat, 2000
+32 (0)488 090 912
lejohn.be

Lunch
Time out

①
Camino, Sint-Andries
Little Asia

This concrete and neon-heavy spot is perennially packed on weekends when reservations are a must. From the epic noodle salad and rice bowls to bahn mi (Vietnamese sandwiches) and slow-roasted pork belly, the menu is a greatest hits of Asian comfort food. We recommend you sample more of it by sharing a liberal array of sides.

If the fresh air out on the terrace and punchy flavours aren't enough to wake you up, order a soju or smoky mezcal cocktail.
4 Muntstraat, 2000
+ 32 (0)3 289 9197
caminoantwerp.com

Must-try
Gourmet fries from Frites Atelier, Historisch Centrum
Far from the humble, retro *fritkot* (chip stand), this marble-adorned temple to the hot chip is run by Michelin-starred chef Sergio Herman (*see page 75*). He uses skin-on potatoes sourced from Holland's Zeeland clay earth, cooked to achieve the ideal soft interior and crunchy exterior. Sauces include shaved-truffle mayo, while toppings span shakshouka and Indonesian peanut.
fritesatelier.com

②
Orso Pizzeria, Zurenborg
Simplicity rules

This superior Italian joint on a Zurenborg street corner reflects owners Isabelle Swaeb and Claudio Leoni's love of simple, high-quality produce. There are only eight pizzas on the menu (with no pineapple in sight), plus natural wines (the house wines are sourced from Leoni's father's vineyard in Emilia Romagna).

Unusually for these parts, every pizza can come gluten-free – a menu quirk that's the result of Swaeb's own lactose and gluten intolerance. "The pizza is a bit browner but you really taste the grain," she says. "Many people without a gluten intolerance prefer it too, which is amazing."
46 Grote Beerstraat, 2018
+ 32 (0)3 501 1177
orsopizzeria.be

③
Native, Sint-Andries
Green haven

Vegetarians and vegans are spoilt for choice at this calm, intimate café. Though Native always offers a meat or fish dish – be it chicken, hummus and almonds on toast by day or Tuscan-style haddock with white beans by night – vegetables are the heroes.

The mismatched decor is anything but superficial. "We started five years ago and didn't want to buy anything new because our philosophy is to reuse," says chef and co-owner Ben Somers. "We took stuff from skips and built new things or went to markets in the south of Belgium. It's one big philosophy with the food – there's already so much waste."
8 Muntstraat, 2000
+32 (0)3 437 0825
native.bio

④
Graanmarkt 13, Theaterbuurt
Noble ingredients

The basement restaurant of this concept store, gallery and apartment (*see pages 70 and 90*) is ideal for a healthy, uncomplicated lunch while browsing the shops. Weather permitting, sit on the terrace where you can admire the classical splendour of the surrounding square, which has hosted a market since the 16th century.

Chef Seppe Nobels transforms whatever is fresh that day into two-course menus featuring fish or meat with tapas-style sides. Nobels' commitment to lowering the ecological footprint of the cuisine is backed up by liberal recourse to his rooftop hives and herb garden.
13 Graanmarkt, 2000
+32 (0)3 337 7991
graanmarkt13.be

Brunch
Pick of the bunch

②
U Eat & Sleep, Eilandje
Port of call

Co-owned by chef Viki Geunes of the two-star 't Zilte in the Mas (*see page 106*) opposite, this cosmopolitan boutique hotel does a good trade in food and drink. While it's best to roll in after overnighting upstairs, wherever you stay it's worth rousing yourself for a bite to eat here along with the priceless views of Eilandje's marina – enjoyed on the terrace, naturally.

Two breakfast menus feature farm eggs and moreish salted green tomatoes alongside artisanal cold cuts. Go à la carte for slightly more decadent options such as smoked salmon with sour cream and dill.
42 Nassaustraat, 2000
+ 32 (0)3 201 9070
u-eatsleep.be

①
Barchel, Klein-Antwerpen
Good looks

"Come for the eye candy, stay for the soul food" is the tagline of this elegant breakfast and lunch spot metres from the Stadspark. While the soul food part is a tad misleading, the smart white tiles, high ceiling and parquet floor nail the visual side of things.

Barchel offers the stuff of salty and sweet brunch dreams, be it Turkish fried eggs in herbed yoghurt or halloumi toast with carrot hummus. It's a real hit with the freelance crowd, who sip potent espressos on the terrace.
6 Van Breestraat, 2018
+ 32 (0)3 501 6416
barchel-antwerp.com

③
Butchers Coffee, Zuid
Aussie rules

An injection of Aussie
café culture in Antwerp,
Dave Haesen's laid-back,
handsomely styled café
occupies (as the name
suggests) an old butcher's
shop. The fare ranges from
the Butchers Breaky (toasted
sourdough, smashed avocado,
poached eggs and labneh) to
eggs Benedict enlivened by
smoked ham hock.

"I lived in Australia for a
couple of years so we were after
that all-day breakfast place vibe
you find there," says Antwerp
native Haesen. "We've very
keen on our music so we
have jazz in the morning then
afternoon hip-hop. We want
to create a natural buzz, like
a bar but by day."
57 Kasteelstraat, 2000
+32 (0)3 334 9193
butcherscoffee.be

Coffee
Better brews

①
Copper, Brederode
Pots and plants

Tucked away in a district
seldom visited by tourists, this
attractive café is well worth
the stroll from the centre.
Impressively it's a one-woman
operation, with chef and owner
Annemiek Visser turning out
tasty tartines alongside superior
coffees, not least the affogato
rich with vanilla ice cream.

The quirky interior feels
distinctly Antwerp in the best
possible way: dictated by
Visser's passions it's a riot of
plants and vintage ceramics,
mostly from the 1950s and
1960s, including birch-bark
pottery with copper glaze.
If anything takes your fancy,
you'll be pleased to hear that
many of the objects are for sale.
80 Belegstraat, 2018
+32 (0)3 291 3060
copper-antwerpen.be

2

Caffènation, Groen Kwartier
Local heroes

"The trouble with speciality coffee is people don't understand what it is," says Rob Berghmans. "There's no perception of where it comes from and how it's harvested, roasted and made."

Since launching Caffènation, Berghmans has battled to change that. He opened his first space in the city centre in 2003 and followed it up with this Groen Kwartier spin-off – home to the brand's roastery – in 2017. "We want to educate people," adds Berghmans. "Last year 700 people came to a coffee class we had here. People know about wine nowadays and if we keep it up thousands will know about coffee too."
161 Lamorinièrestraat, 2018
+ 32 (0)3 501 2292
caffenation.be

3

Normo, Historisch Centrum
Strong views and brews

They take their coffee very seriously at this elegantly dishevelled café between the city centre and Red Light District. While you'll find just about every kind of non-dairy milk going, the proper Normo way is to go black, whether with the automatic filter version or – making like barista Jens Oris – the more sophisticated slow-drip V60 Hario. Rare Silver Needle blends are part of the selection by top Belgian tea sommelier Ann Vansteenkiste. Remember to bring cash: no foreign cards accepted.
30 Minderbroedersrui, 2000
+ 32 (0)495 657 243
normocoffee.be

1

Domestic Bakkerij, Zurenborg
Forget Paris

Originally owned by Antwerp restaurant Dôme and its fish-centric sibling (*see page 76*) – both of which still favour its bread – this is the city's most celebrated bakery.

The marble counter displays refined, surprisingly light patisserie, from revelatory pistachio eclairs to raspberry tarts piled high with fruit, and you'll also find a dizzying selection of artisanal bread. If this is slightly out of the way, opt for the city-centre branch whose pastel-pink salon serves a tasty English-style high tea.
37 Steenbokstraat, 2018
+ 32 (0)3 239 9890
domestic-bakkerij.be

②
Bakkerij Goossens, Historisch Centrum
Analogue charm

Snaking queues attest to the quality of Antwerp's oldest bakery, in action since 1884. It's now run by the fourth generation and continues to do a swift trade in pastries, *bokkenpootje* (chocolate-dipped macaroon-style almond cookies with butter cream) and, most famously, *roggeverdommeke* (rye bread studded with raisins).

"The *speculoos* (a type of spiced biscuit) is based on the recipe of my great-great-grandfather, who founded the bakery, and the mould in which it's baked is the original," says Laura Goossens. Don't expect to find a website or social media account. "We're very much set on being authentic and analogue," she adds.
31 Korte Gasthuisstraat, 2000
+32 (0)3 226 0791

Sweet spots

01 Hoeked, Theaterbuurt: This doughnut parlour's brioche creations are rectangular rather than round – but there's far more going on here than shapely gimmicks. Doughnutier Joris Verschelden experiments with spelt and multigrain mixtures and different flavours. Try the SaltySweet, dipped in caramel and finished with sprinkles of Ibizan salt.
hoekeddoughnuts.be

02 Philip's Biscuits, Historisch Centrum: Top draw at the city's biscuit king are the shortbread *Antwerpse handjes* (Antwerp Hands). The moniker – and the name of the city – stems from a legend involving a giant called Druon Antigoon and the Roman centurion who cut off his hand. Nothing like a backstory with bite.
philipsbiscuits.be

③
Bakker Aldo, Groen Kwartier
Honest bread

Opened in 2015 by a graduate of Domestic Bakkerij (*see page 83*), this bakery made waves with its focus on authentic French methods: artisanal bread consisting of nothing more than flour, water and salt, plus yeast or sourdough. "It's an honest product made with love and care," says Sheena De Pauw, who took over the venture with her brother in 2019. "At other bakeries they add butter and things to make the flour stay fresh longer. It's difficult to do without but that's what we stand for."
388 Lange Leemstraat, 2018
+32 (0)3 239 2125
bakkeraldo.be

Drinks
Setting a bar

①
Vitrin, Zuid
Meeting place

This corner café morphs into an aperitivo hotspot come early evening and is a popular rendezvous point for local fashion and design players. There's no table service so head into the compact wooden interior to order.

Opt for an Aperol Spritz if the sun is out or, slightly more adventurously, a Cynar and white wine; the menu also includes a decent array of beers and non-alcoholic wines. The most in-demand tables are back outside, overlooking the attractive Marnixplaats.
14 Marnixplaats, 2000
vitrin.eu

Nice *apretiv… aprivi… drink*

②

Belgian Wines, Theaterbuurt
Fine vintage

South Belgium is now producing high-quality wines with soil akin to Champagne some 10 years ago (whites and sparkling wine are standouts). "Sommeliers really like to work with Belgian wines because they're new, special and exclusive," says Koen De Bock, who runs this Theaterbuurt stop-in together with brothers Jens and Jonas De Maere.

Top-tier names such as Clos d'Opleeuw are on offer at Belgian Wines, which the De Maeres launched online in 2011 before opening a bricks-and-mortar space in 2015. It also serves fine cheese and charcuterie. Visit on a Saturday and you'll find the city's best food market out front.
24 Oudevaartplaats, 2000
+ 32 (0)3 755 8755
belgianwines.com

③

Dogma Cocktails, Historisch Centrum
Rich mix

The chances of remaining sober at this speakeasy-style cocktail joint are slim. Better to go with the flow, which means surrendering to a creative libation – the hefty price tag will be worth it – and retreating to a Chesterfield.

When it comes to choosing you can't really go wrong, though the bartenders are on hand to make suggestions if you need. Those of a more venturesome persuasion should investigate the Aix en Provence, a potent fruity mix of apple brandy, honey, thyme, citrus and goat's cheese foam (it works, we promise).
5 Wijngaardstraat, 2000
+ 32 (0)3 770 6477
dogmacocktails.be

Historic hangouts

01 De Vagant, Historisch Centrum: Most people associate jenever with the Dutch but in centuries past there were dozens of distilleries devoted to the spirit – a juniper-infused gin prototype – in Antwerp. This very friendly café has been keeping its memory alive for decades, with the current location (opened in 1985) hosting a small upstairs museum on local jenever history. Sample some 220 types in the café then buy a bottle to take away.
devagant.be

02 Café De Kat, Historisch Centrum: From the mahogany walls to the neon De Koninck sign, this classic brown bar is a historic gem. It's popular with Antwerp artists, many of an advanced age, and a wonderfully anti-commercial spirit extends to the uncompromising drinks list – which features, for example, either "red wine" or "the good red".
+32 (0)3 233 0892

03 De Plek, Historisch Centrum: Knocking back a cold beer inside a Unesco-listed cathedral (the Rubens-rich Cathedral of Our Lady) is among the more unusual things to do in town. Set in the former Saint John's Chapel, this gothic-inspired bar is the only place where you can drink dark and blonde beers produced for the site by a local brewery.
dekathedraal.be

Retail
—— Shop talk

Antwerp is home to one of Europe's most prosperous ports and its enviable roster of independent retailers reflects a long and industrious history of import and export. The city may have made a name for itself through the diamond trade but beyond the glittering jewellery shops you'll find plenty of other gems.

The emergence of the Antwerp Six in the mid-1980s put the city on the sartorial map and, since then, Antwerp's homegrown fashion scene has continued to go from strength to strength.

We've rounded up our favourite retail outposts, from a bookshop on the ground floor of an art deco school to a glove shop that has been keeping hands elegant and cosy since 1884. Expect sleek showrooms and sharp branding across the board: this is a city that knows how to make you part with your pennies – and look good in the process.

Fashion
Clothes on

①
Arte, Sint-Andries
Cool character

The brainchild of graphic designer Bertony Da Silva, Arte started out in 2009 as a capsule T-shirt collection inspired by music, art, architecture and graphic design. Today it's a fully fledged menswear brand, which has added a touch of cool to Kammenstraat's retail offering since the shop opened in 2016.

"Our collections are rooted in Antwerp's street culture, with a nod to classic cuts and workwear," says Da Silva. Everything is designed in the Antwerp studio.
54 Kammenstraat, 2000
+32 (0)471 918 325
arte-antwerp.com

②
Dries Van Noten, Historisch Centrum
Leader of the pack

Arguably Antwerp's most famous fashion export, Dries Van Noten was born into a local family of tailors. A graduate of the city's Royal Academy of Fine Arts and a member of the Antwerp Six (*see pages 88 and 130*), he opened his first boutique in his hometown in 1986.

Three years later Van Noten moved into this art nouveau former department store on a narrow corner of the Nationalestraat, which acts as the flagship for his now internationally lauded brand. His trademark bold colours, rich fabrics and punchy patterns are artfully arranged across all five floors.
16 Nationalestraat, 2000
+32 (0)3 470 2510
driesvannoten.be

❸
Morrison, Sint-Andries
Mini marvel

"Small is beautiful," says Patrick Olyslager, who, together with his brother Jan, deliberately sought a diminutive space for his menswear shop in order to create intimacy and ensure the tightest edit of products. "The brands are selected based on their quality, longevity and finesse," he adds. "Where the product comes from and how it's made is paramount to the selection process."

Labels that make the cut include A Kind of Guise, Beams Plus, Universal Works and Howlin', an Antwerp-based knitwear brand that makes many of its pieces in Belgium. There's also a (small) range of records, books and accessories.
20 Nationalestraat, 2000
+ 32 (0)3 322 1851
morrison.be

Luxury threads
———
Housed in two adjoining townhouses and lit by an elegant zodiac-themed glass dome, Verso is the city's best-stocked fashion-led department store. This is your best bet for all the big names such as Dolce & Gabbana, Valentino and Fendi.
verso.com

④
Ann Demeulemeester, Zuid
Black and white

Another member of the
Antwerp Six (*see right and page
130*), Ann Demeulemeester
established her fashion house
in 1985 and opened this
lofty flagship in 1999. The
walls are wrapped in white
canvas – a fitting backdrop
for Demeulemeester's striking
silhouettes and sharp cuts.

Demeulemeester passed
the baton to artistic director
Sebastien Meunier in 2013
but you can expect the same
signature look: namely a
rebellious, rock aesthetic with
delicate detailing inspired by the
frills and cuffs so popular with
the Romantic poets. Colour is
in short supply here – both the
collections for men and women
are resolutely monochrome.
*Leopold de Waelplaats, 2000
+ 32 (0)3 216 0133
anndemeulemeester.com*

The A team

Talk about fashion in Antwerp
and it won't be long before the
Antwerp Six crop up. Dries Van
Noten, Ann Demeulemeester,
Dirk Van Saene, Walter Van
Beirendonck, Dirk Bikkembergs
and Marina Yee formed one
of the most influential fashion
collectives of all time (*see
page 130*).

5

Enes, Zuid
Storied space

Ghent-born Muriel Van Nieuwenhove opened her first pop-up shop at the age of 18 on the Belgian coast. After a stint working for the Belgian brand Scapa she founded Enes in 2000 and the brand has been based in this historic townhouse since 2015: "It has been a famous bar, a restaurant, a hotel and an antique shop: if the walls could talk they could write a book," she says.

It's the perfect setting for the shop's range of mixed-label womenswear. The bold design by Gert Voorjans preserves the domestic feel of the building: you'll find a bathroom stocked with beauty products and the original Cubex kitchen replete with accessories and candles.
58 Volkstraat, 2000
+32 (0)3 227 4693
enes.be

Tinker tailor
—
Café Costume takes an à la carte approach to tailoring. Customers can choose from countless high-quality materials and buttons – many from Italy and France – to design a truly made-to-measure suit. Call in advance for an appointment.
cafecostume.com

6

Louis, Historisch Centrum
Host with the most

From its infancy, Louis has hosted Antwerp's most important fashion designers. Founded in 1986 by Geert Bruloot and Eddy Michiels – and now run under the watchful eye of Marjan Eggers, who joined the team back in 1990 – the shop showed the first collections from Ann Demeulemeester (*see opposite*) and Martin Margiela.

"I started working here while still a student," says Eggers. "There were clothes in the window I'd never experienced in my entire life – I was mesmerised." Today Louis has a more international outlook, with staples from Acne Studios and Balenciaga alongside the usual Belgian suspects.
2 Lombardenstraat, 2000
+32 (0)3 232 9872
louisantwerp.be

①

St Vincents, Theaterbuurt
New lease of life

When Henri Delbarre and
Geraldine Jackman gave up
their office jobs to take the lease
on this former printing house
in 2015 there was no water,
electricity or flooring and
the walls were splashed with
graffiti. Things have changed
a little since then.

An industrial feel prevails
but the space is now the
picture of understated
elegance. You'll find furniture,
art and design from brands
such as Apparatus Studio
and Santa & Cole, as well
as pieces by young Belgian
designers including woodwork
artist Kaspar Hamacher and
ceramicist Alex Gabriels.
There is also a café area
serving coffee from Brussels-
based Mok (*see page 29*).
13 Kleine Markt, 2000
stvincents.co

②

Graanmarkt 13, Theaterbuurt
All in one

Designed by Belgian architect
Vincent Van Duysen,
Graanmarkt 13 combines
homeware, fashion and
accessories with a downstairs
restaurant (*see page 80*) and
a top-floor rental apartment
(*see page 70*) in a grand
neoclassical townhouse. When
founders Tim Van Geloven
and Ilse Cornelissens opened
in 2010 they set out to create
a place where everyone would
feel at home.

The couple naturally
drift towards national
and smaller brands. Two
weekends a year customers
can exchange used clothing for
store credit, which the team
considers a fair and fresh
way to honour sustainability.
13 Graanmarkt, 2000
+32 (0)3 337 7992
graanmarkt13.com

Homeware
In the house

①

Studio Helder, Kievitwijk
Inside job

With a changing line-up of brands from Belgium and beyond, Diana Keller and Brecht Baert's (*pictured*) shop showcases their services as interior designers. "There's always been an interest in fashion in Antwerp but now there's more talk about design and interiors too," says Keller.

The pair's focus lies with independent designers who produce on a small scale. You'll find their own creations – such as tables and lamps – alongside jewellery by Stephanie Schneider and furniture by Muller Van Severen. "We see our shop as a 3D business card, where we can interact naturally with our customers," says Baert.
100 Provinciestraat, 2018
+ 32 (0)3 289 4318
studiohelder.be

③

Atelier Solarshop, Seefhoek
Tried and tested

This independent space in the lively Seefhoek district was founded by Piëtro Celestina and Jan-Jan Van Essche in 2008 and started out as an experimental space for art, design, fashion and food. It evolved into a more traditional shop in 2012 and now carries jewellery, art, vintage furniture and pieces from Van Essche's own fashion line.

The interior of the shop – which is housed in a former solar panel store, hence the name – is constantly evolving as the duo hunt and collect one-off pieces on their travels: "At the moment it has a very Japanese-meets-West African feel," says Celestina. "But who knows for how long."
48 Dambruggestraat, 2060
+ 32 (0)487 167 570
ateliersolarshop.be

②
Espoo, Sint-Andries
Scandi style

Dries Brys (*pictured*) attributes his interest in product design to childhood trips spent accompanying his father to glass and mirror factories across Europe. Back in his native Belgium he spotted a gap in the market for a one-stop shop carrying Nordic homeware. "I founded the shop in 2009," he says. "It felt like the right time to introduce Belgians to the new Nordic design brands that I discovered on my travels and couldn't find in any other shop here."

Espoo has stayed true to its roots. Flanked by the antique shops of Kloosterstraat it is a beacon of Scandi cool, stocking classic pieces by Artek, Frama, Muuto and more.
75-77 Kloosterstraat, 2000
+ 32 (0)3 237 5797
espoo.be

③
Magazyn, Historisch Centrum
Part of the furniture

After years spent working in visual merchandising and art direction, Thomas Haarmann decided it was time to put the focus back on craft. He had noticed that many of his clients were looking for a company offering high-quality, handcrafted pieces – and that's exactly what you'll find at Magazyn, his pitch-perfect space on Steenhouwersvest.

The concrete-heavy showroom displays Haarmann's own furniture range and changes appearance relatively frequently. "There has to be a flow in the shop but we keep our basic collection," he says. "And it has to reflect our philosophy of slowing down and less consumption."
34A Steenhouwersvest, 2000
+ 32 (0)3 226 6606
magazyn.be

**Specialist retail
One-hit wonders**

①
Baltimore Bloemen, Theaterbuurt
Best blooms

Whether you're in the market for a single handpicked bloom or a full shopfront display, our choice for all things floral is Baltimore Bloemen. With more than 25 years experience in the industry, florist Mark Colle's buds and bouquets are Antwerp's finest.

"I guess my mission statement would be: flowers for everyone," says Colle (*pictured*). "I've been lucky enough to work with giant fashion houses and do larger-than-life weddings, but I'm just as happy in my shop, helping that nervous kid on a second date who has €12 to spend on something."
6 Orgelstraat, 2000
+ 32 (0)3 232 2838
baltimorebloemen.be

Natty outfit? Check. Beautiful flowers? Check. Someone to give flowers to? Ah

②
Juwelenhuis Ruys, Theaterbuurt
Diamonds in the sky

More than 80 per cent of the world's rough diamonds pass through Antwerp, so it's no surprise the city is packed with jewellery shops. The oldest in town – in fact, reportedly in the country – is this gem overseen by fifth-generation owner Jean Van der Haegen (*pictured*). Juwelenhuis Ruys first opened its doors in 1854 and has purveyed its jewellery, watches and silverware ever since.

The shop is worth a visit for the space alone: the shopfront dates back to 1902 and is an art nouveau triumph. Inside, the mosaic floors, painted ceilings, mirrored cabinets and art deco lighting almost outshine the precious stones on display.
26 Sint-Jorispoort, 2000
+ 32 (0)3 232 4965
ruys.be

③
Ganterie Boon, Historisch Centrum
Fits like a glove

Founded in 1884 by two Italian brothers, this pocket-sized *ganterie* (glove shop) stocks some 8,000 pairs of leather gloves and hasn't changed much since the oak-panelled interiors were installed in the late 1920s – even the old till survives. "I never thought about altering it," says the shop's former owner Patsy Sarteel. She manned the counters from the mid-1970s until passing on the reins to her daughter, fourth-generation owner Sofie Possemiers (*pictured*), who can judge a hand size by sight.

We'd recommend inquiring about a toasty hand-stitched, sheepskin-lined pair.
2 Lombardenvest, 2000
+ 32 (0)3 232 3387
glovesboon.be

Little one
—
Komono is Japanese for "small things" and it's safe to say that this Antwerp brand gets the little things right. Founded in 2009 by Belgian designers Raf Maes and Anton Janssens, it offers a chic range of affordable eyewear and watches designed in the city.
komono.com

②
Copyright, Sint-Andries
Art et al

Copyright's large glass door offers passage to perhaps the city's best space for books. The brainchild of Antwerp-born art historian Hilde Peleman (who opened the original and ever popular Copyright in Ghent back in 1983), it has offered a haven on the busy Nationalestraat since 2001. "We moved to Nationalestraat at the request of Linda Loppa, the former director of Momu," says Peleman. "She wanted us there because we would not be a typical museum shop, with gadgets and knick-knacks, but a fully-fledged bookshop."

Head here for monographs, magazines and coffee-table books heavy on architecture, art, fashion and design.
28A Nationalestraat, 2000
+ 32 (0)3 232 9416
copyrightbookshop.be

①
Cronopio, Theaterbuurt
Old school

Housed on the ground floor of Sint-Lievenscollege – a late-1920s art deco school building which unusually had purpose-built retail spaces incorporated into the original design – this smart bookshop-cum-café was opened by Ine Schepmans in 2015. The offering is roughly split 50-50 between English and Dutch titles, which cover fiction, art, photography and cooking, as well as a charming selection of books for nippers.

The inspiration for the name comes from a novel by Argentinian author Julio Cortázar, explains Schepmans. "In general a *cronopio* is someone who goes against the current but always in a friendly manner."
21 Kasteelpleinstraat, 2000
+ 32 (0)3 226 6894
cronopio.be

*Another
Aperol
Spritz?
Sure!*

Culture
—— Small
but mighty

Museums and public galleries
Must-see institutions

What Antwerp lacks in size, it makes up for with its cultural landscape. With envelope-pushing gallerists, a handful of interdisciplinary arts centres and a museum displaying a collection from one of the world's foremost fashion academies, there's plenty on offer for a spectrum of tastes. Though at the time of going to press several venues were closed for renovation work, this only testifies to a scene that's both growing and gaining international stature.

It's the cutting-edge creative scene that really makes the city what it is. With a housing market still lagging behind big artistic bastions such as London and Amsterdam, Antwerp's affordability and laid-back lifestyle remains attractive for young European artists looking for space to create.

So come delve into this unpretentious nest of experimental music, visual arts, arthouse film and bricolage.

①
M HKA, Zuid
Local favourite

This contemporary-art hub celebrates everything from Flanders' postwar avant garde tradition to today's most prominent artists. Its permanent collection includes pieces from notable Belgian artists – including Jan Fabre, Jef Geys, Panamarenko and Luc Tuymans – and international artists such as Marlene Dumas, Marina Abramovic and Gordon Matta-Clark.

The museum plays host to talks, screenings and concerts, and since being renovated in 2017 the former grain silo also houses a cosy café, a sunny roof terrace and a tranquil foyer designed by Axel Vervoordt (*see page 99*) and Tatsuro Miki.
32 Leuvenstraat, 2000
+ 32 (0)3 260 9999
muhka.be

I'm
very
present
in my
art

2

Middelheimmuseum,
Middelheim
En plein air

When the sun decides to
make an appearance, pack a
picnic and hop on a tram to
this picturesque alfresco art
and sculpture museum. It
was first opened in 1951 and
today its park is dotted with
more than 215 permanent
sculptures by artists such as
Auguste Rodin, Henry Moore,
Ai Weiwei, Barbara Hepworth
and Bruce Nauman. Each
year the museum invites artists
to create new site-specific
sculptures, which has resulted
in collaborations with Adrien
Tirtiaux, Erwin Wurm, William
Forsythe and more.

    Don't miss the Renaat
Braem-designed pavilion, used
for temporary exhibitions, and
be sure to spend some time
strolling the 27 hectares of leafy
parkland – a prime example
of landscape art.
*61 Middelheimlaan, 2020
+ 32 (0)3 288 3360
middelheimmuseum.be*

Three more museums

01 Mas, Eilandje: Within this boxy architectural icon by Neutelings Riedijk Architects (*see page 106*) you'll find objects and photos telling the story of Antwerp's glory years as a port city. Temporary exhibitions vary from Le Corbusier's unrealised plans for Antwerp's left bank and the first retrospective of Belgian baroque artist Michaelina Wautier to Japanese popular culture. Head to the top for a 360-degree panoramic view of the city and the Schelde.
mas.be

02 Fomu, Zuid: Located in an imposing former warehouse a stone's throw from both M HKA (*see page 96*) and KMSKA (*see below*), Antwerp's photography museum contains an impressive collection of works by big-name snappers such as Henri-Cartier Bresson, Man Ray and Irving Penn. Since its inception in 1965, it has helped to promote Zuid as the museum district par excellence.
fotomuseum.be

03 KMSKA, Zuid: At the time of writing, the Royal Museum of Fine Arts Antwerp (commonly known as KMSKA) is set to re-open in 2020 after nine years of renovation work. Head to the imposing neoclassical building to walk among works by Flemish masters such as James Ensor and Peter Paul Rubens.
kmska.be

③
Rubenshuis, Historisch Centrum
Solo show

In Antwerp's old town, the former residence of famous Flemish artist Peter Paul Rubens provides a glimpse of what life was like in the golden age. Reminiscent of the architecture of Italian palazzos, Rubenshuis exudes Rubens' artistic ideals: the art of Roman antiquity and the Italian renaissance.

Highlights include the artist's spectacular studio – complete with his famous self-portrait, head tilted in a wide-brimmed hat – and the garden with its restored portico and pavilion. Stroll over to a bench and sit for a while in what is undoubtedly one of Antwerp's best hideaways.
9-11 Wapper, 2000
+ 32 (0)3 201 1555
rubenshuis.be

④
ModeMuseum, Sint-Andries
Belgian style

At the time of writing, Antwerp's fashion museum (Momu) is undergoing renovation and plans to re-open in 2021. The main objective is to refurbish the current exhibition spaces and create a new home for the permanent collection – comprising some 30,000 pieces – to better tell the story of Antwerp's central position in the canon of global fashion.

The entrance hall designed by Marie-José Van Hee will be preserved, its sculptural wooden staircase snaking through the building from the museum to the famous fashion academy, where eccentrically dressed students saunter past curious visitors. While the institution is closed, check the website for temporary exhibitions at alternative locations or book the guided Momu Fashion Walk.
28 Nationalestraat, 2000
+ 32 (0)3 470 2770
momu.be

I've always had a good eye for fashion

Commercial galleries
Creative enterprise

(1)
Axel Vervoordt Gallery,
Wijnegem
Out of the white box

In 2017, Axel Vervoordt moved
his gallery into Kanaal (*see
page 105*), a former distillery
and malting complex that he
converted into a whopping
development. Its jaw-dropping
spaces – the light-flooded
Patio Gallery, the pitch-black
Terrace Gallery and the
industrial Escher Gallery –
host temporary exhibitions.
Past shows have focused on
works by the likes of Ilya and
Emilia Kabakov, Japanese
Gutai group's Yuko Nasaka
and Renato Nicolodi.

Pieces from the permanent
collection of the Axel & May
Vervoordt Foundation can
be seen upon reservation:
Anish Kapoor's "At the Edge
of the World", James Turrell's
"Red Shift" and works by
Kimsooja, Tatsuo Miyajima,
Takis, Bosco Sodi and more.
Defying the ubiquitous white-
cube approach, Vervoordt's
philosophy – in which timeless
architecture, art and nature
become one – culminates here
at Kanaal. Not to be missed.
19 Stokerijstraat, 2110
+ 32 (0)3 355 3300
axel-vervoordt.com

②
Zeno X Gallery, Borgerhout
Breaking new ground

Zeno X, one of Belgium's most established private galleries, took a risk in 2013 when it moved from trendy Zuid to a former milk factory in the northern district of Borgerhout. Since then, it's played a major role in the neighbourhood's emerging creative spirit, which now draws young artists.

The gallery represents acclaimed Belgian creators such as Michaël Borremans, Luc Tuymans and Anne-Mie Van Kerckhoven, as well as the likes of Marlene Dumas and Anton Corbijn.
15 Godtsstraat, 2140
+32 (0)3 216 1626
zeno-x.com

③
Valerie Traan Gallery, Historisch Centrum
Creative worship

This commercial venture opened in 2010 to showcase the best of Belgian and international design talent, from the acclaimed duo Muller Van Severen to 3D ceramicists Unfold. The former convent – with well-lit white walls, lofty ceilings and original brick floors – dates back to 1979.

The interplay between good design, architecture and art is at the heart of owner Veerle Wenes' ethos and life; she lives in an adjoining house, also filled with art and design objects.
12 Reyndersstraat, 2000
+32 (0)475 759 459
valerietraan.be

Cultural centres and cinemas
Mixed-media hubs

①
DeSingel, Markgrave
Interdisciplinary musings

Since it opened in 1980, DeSingel has been breaking down barriers between disciplines. The building itself is worth perusing: Léon Stynen's modernist shell stands in stark contrast to architect Stéphane Beel's 2007 extension.

Come to see everything from contemporary dance and theatre to music concerts and architecture exhibitions. Past performances have been led by choreographer Anne Teresa De Keersmaeker and theatre director Robert Wilson.
25 Desguinlei, 2018
+ 32 (0)3 248 2828
desingel.be

④
Tim Van Laere Gallery, Zuid
Breeding ground

This renowned contemporary-art gallery moved to Nieuw Zuid, a low-impact urban-development project, in 2019. Designed by Brussels-based Office Kersten Geers David Van Severen, the concrete space aims to contribute to the local area and the city at large by making exhibitions – and, by extension, art – accessible.

Since 1997, Tim Van Laere has built a reputation for being a visionary powerhouse and nurturing fresh talent. The roster bears some of the most exciting names in Europe. Keep an eye out for Belgians Rinus Van de Velde and Ben Sledsens, and international artists Adrian Ghenie and Jonathan Meese.
50 Jos Smolderenstraat, 2000
+ 32 (0)3 257 1417
timvanlaeregallery.com

Cinema Cartoon's,
Historisch Centrum
Devoted clientele

This small cinema opened
in 1978 and has since been
spared closure more than
once by a loyal crowd of
cinephiles. In 2014 it received
investment from arthouse
film distributor Lumière.

A selection of European
films, US indie flicks and
documentaries show in three
cosy screening rooms. As soon
as the film credits roll, flock to
the bar in the basement of this
former chocolate factory for
an extensive beer and wine
list and occasional live music.
*4-6 Kaasstraat, 2000
+ 32 (0)3 232 9632
cinemacartoons.be*

De Roma, Borgerhout
Community mainstay

Visitors are drawn to this
concert hall for its breathtaking
architecture as much as its
impeccable programming.
When it was built in 1928, the
art deco cinema was the largest
playhouse in town; it enjoyed
another heyday in the 1960s
and 1970s with stars such as
Lou Reed and Iggy Pop taking
to its stage. De Roma closed
in 1982 but 20 years later was
restored to its former grandeur.

Supported by volunteers, the
hall is today the beating heart
of its diverse neighbourhood.
In addition to live music riffing
across the musical spectrum,
it offers documentaries, talks
and festivals. A visit serves as
an excellent introduction to
this vibrant pocket of the city.
*286 Turnhoutsebaan, 2140
+ 32 (0)3 600 1660
deroma.be*

Day and night
──
The multipurpose, not-for-
profit Het Bos offers artist
residencies, a culturally diverse
programme of film and musical
performances, and a bar
selling snacks and organic
beers. It's also known for its
nightlife; parties go on into
the early hours.
hetbos.be

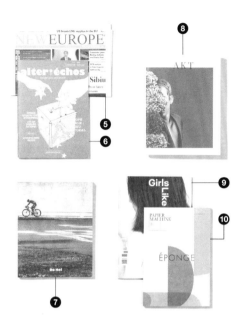

① Media
What to read

Belgium has its fair share of print publications, partly because the country caters to both French and Dutch-language readers. Kiosks and shops selling newspapers and magazines are dotted around Brussels and Antwerp.

One of the highest-quality Flemish newspapers is ❶ *De Standaard*, a daily tabloid with a sharp world-news section. The salmon-pink ❷ *De Tijd* is based in Brussels and, like other rosy-shaded papers around the world, focuses predominantly on business and economics. ❸ *De Morgen* sits alongside *De Standaard* in terms of quality, and has a fine online presence. The French-language ❹ *Le Soir* is a daily that includes everything from culture and sports coverage to weather and traffic information.

For English speakers (and those with a keen interest in the EU), the Brussels-based weekly ❺ *New Europe* reports on the latest news from EU institutions. ❻ *Alter Échos* is a monthly publication from Agence Alter, an agency that specialises in social research, and explores economics in 21st-century society.

Moving onto more niche publications, ❼ *Bahamontes* is a quarterly magazine that reports on all things cycling, with snappy write-ups and stellar photography. ❽ *AKT* is a tastefully put together tome – with a *Cereal*-esque eye for design – that covers fashion, food, architecture and more. Through personal stories and avant garde images, ❾ *Girls Like Us* shines a spotlight on women involved in art, culture and activism. And finally, the Brussels-based ❿ *Papier Machine* is devoted to all things linguistics.

Radio

Here are two independent Belgian stations to tune into.

01 Radio Centraal: Online or 106.7FM is where you'll find Antwerp's Radio Centraal, a volunteer-run independent that plays experimental music, from obscure pop and surf rock to catchy popcorn and cult-movie soundtracks.
radiocentraal.be

02 The Word Radio: The radio branch of the former magazine by the same name broadcasts 24/7 and champions often-overlooked underground talent, giving some 100 monthly residents a platform for DJ sets and mixtapes.
theword.radio

Design and architecture
—— Mixed bag

Antwerp is well balanced when it comes to architecture, with a healthy mix of old and new. From the Grote Markt, whose 16th-century renaissance-style town hall and guild houses are evocative of the golden age, to 21st-century gems dotted around the docks, Antwerp will surprise and delight.

The port city is peppered with historic churches and cavernous warehouses, many of which have been repurposed as concert halls and cultural archives while retaining their charm. It's about as relaxed as they come but should you need extra peace and quiet, stroll among the breathtaking art nouveau mansions in Zurenborg.

Contemporary architecture is progressive yet sensitively produced, the result of restoration and reimagination. Since 2000, sparkling new creations designed by international talent and homegrown luminaries have punctuated the landscape, including Zaha Hadid's glistening Havenhuis. The best way to see it all is by bike, so join us for a pedal.

①

Havenhuis, Eilandje
Starry port

As Europe's second-largest shipping port, it's only fitting that Antwerp has a *havenhuis* (port house) worthy of the name. The late, great Zaha Hadid repurposed the former fire station as a new headquarters for the city's Port Authority between 2009 and 2016, bringing together 500 members of staff who previously worked in different buildings dotted around the city.

Supported by a central circulation tower and an angular concrete crutch, Hadid's 111-metre-long glass extension is elevated above the original heritage-listed building like a ship ready to launch. In the light, the triangular panels on its façade (half transparent, half opaque) appear to ripple like waves – or, somewhat appropriately for Antwerp, sparkle like diamonds.
1 Zaha Hadidplein, 2030

②
Kanaal, Wijnegem
Industry movements

Belgian interior designer and collector Axel Vervoordt (*see page 99*) drew on years of experience to create Kanaal, a new cultural, commercial and residential development. The project was two decades in the making and has seen a ruined industrial site transformed into something of a self-sufficient vertical village.

"The old building is something I really love and that is why we added contemporary architecture that forms a dialogue with it, rather than overpowers it," says Vervoordt, who developed the project with his two sons Boris and Dickie. Architects were invited to work on different parts of the site: Coussée & Goris extended the old buildings and Stéphane Beel transformed the grain towers. "We worked closely with Bogdan & Van Broeck to create something that was not too modern, something that harked back to the Roman period," adds Vervoordt. "The result is not designer architecture – it's interesting and lively architecture."
19 Stokerijstraat, 2110
+ 32 (0)3 355 3800
kanaal.be

❸

Mas, Eilandje
Instant icon

Antwerp's municipal museum, Museum aan de Stroom (Mas), teeters on the edge of the harbour like a Jenga tower about to topple. The nine-storey structure of offset boxes is held steady by giant steel trusses that are visible within the cantilevered galleries. The wave-like windows were constructed from fluted glass made in Verona and the red sandstone (of which there are four shades) was sourced from four quarries in Rajasthan.

Designed by Neutelings Riedijk Architects on the site of the former German Trading Federation HQ and warehouse, Mas gave the city an architectural icon when it opened in 2011. The metal ornaments on the façade take the shape of hands, the symbol of the city, and a window on the fifth floor offers views of the "Dead Skull" mosaic by Luc Tuymans in the square. Luckily neither upstage the 470,000 pieces housed within the museum, which tell the story of Antwerp.
*1 Hanzestedenplaats, 2000
+ 32 (0)3 338 4400
mas.be*

If I mess this up there could be a Mas exodus

⑤

Antwerpen Justitiepaleis, Zuid
High-flying design

A competition was held in 1999 to select a design for a new Palace of Justice. The winning architect was Richard Rogers, and his law court opened in 2006.

The five-storey structure, designed with Belgian firm VK Studio, is capped with a striking sail-like roof. A whopping wooden staircase provides access to the central hall, which is crowned with a glass roof intended to symbolise the transparency of the Belgian judicial system. Six wings clad in shimmering steel radiate out from the centre; from the ground they resemble shark fins and from above, less menacingly, a butterfly – hence the nickname, Vlinderpaleis (Butterfly Palace).
20 Bolivarplaats, 2000

Pakt, Groen Kwartier
Creative hub

This development of beautifully renovated three-storey buildings is sandwiched between the luxury real-estate project Groen Kwartier (Green Quarter) and Antwerp's historic Jewish neighbourhood. Brothers Yusuf and Ismaïl Yaman bought the abandoned construction yard in 2006 and, with the help of entrepreneur Stefan Bostoen, transformed it into a hub for creative businesses that launched in 2017.

The team worked with Belgian architect Roel Vermeesch to turn the derelict warehouses into workspaces. They kept many original features, including the concrete window frames, and made some heritage additions such as an old bridge that now hangs above the courtyard. The cherry on top: rooftop vegetable gardens – the largest of their kind in Belgium.
1 Regine Beerplein, 2018
pakt-antwerpen.be

On your bike

Antwerp is made for cycling (*see pages 67 and 114*) and Visit Antwerp has devised a 30km cycling route that will take you past everything from these contemporary gems to modernist houses and the renaissance town hall. Pick up a map at a visitor centre.
visitantwerpen.be

⑥
Sint-Felix Pakhuis, Eilandje
Out of ashes

This warehouse complex was erected in 1858 according to a design by Belgian architect Félix Pauwels. Three years later it burned down and was rebuilt with materials salvaged from the rubble, except this time a central arcade was added under a glass roof, dividing the building in two.

Originally used to store goods such as coffee and cheese, Sint-Felix Pakhuis was abandoned when the port activity shifted to more sizeable docks. It was pronounced a protected monument in 1976 and now contains the city council's municipal archives.
30 Godefriduskaai, 2000

20th century
Fresh thinking

①
Sint-Annatunnel
Underwater thoroughfare

Unlike other major riverside cities, there are no historical bridges in Antwerp. In fact, there are no bridges at all. The Schelde is the lifeblood of this port city and any 20th-century proposals for a bridge that might obstruct ships passing through were met with a definite *neen*. Instead, the journey from city centre to Linkeroever (Left Bank) starts with a subterranean ride on a set of atmospheric, if slightly creaky, wooden escalators.

The 572-metre-long pedestrian passage opened in 1933 and is still almost completely original, from the switches and safety signs to the cream-coloured ceramic tiles. The two yellow-brick buildings by which you enter and emerge were designed by architect Emiel Van Averbeke in the style of new pragmatism, a Dutch period of modernist architecture characterised by angular shapes.

②
Huis Van Roosmalen,
Sint-Andries
Earned its stripes

When Bob Van Reeth was commissioned to create a home for the interior designer Will Van Roosmalen in 1985, he gifted Antwerp one of its most exuberant private residences.

Inspired by the Viennese modernist Adolf Loos's unbuilt house for the dancer Josephine Baker, it distorts the original's modernist geometries into a postmodernist funhouse. Irregularly sized windows and diagonally jutting levels gesture towards surrealism, while a pair of circular portholes and a ship-like upper floor pay tribute to Antwerp's nautical history.
*Corner of Sint-Michielskaai and Goedehoopstraat, 2000
awg.be*

Into the mix
—
The Zurenborg neighbourhood (*see page 116*) is home to the finest flowering of neoclassical, neo-gothic and, above all, art nouveau houses in Belgium. Saunter along the Cogels-Osylei and soak up the enchanting late-19th and early 20th-century residences.

Tower types

01 **Boerentoren, Historisch Centrum:** If you're in need of a landmark to help you navigate look to the centrally located Boerentoren (Farmers' Tower). Designed by Belgian architect Jan Vanhoenacker and built ahead of Antwerp's 1930 World Exhibition, the art deco structure – officially known as the KBC Tower – is said to have been Europe's first skyscraper.
35 Schoenmarkt, 2000

02 **BP Building, Tentoonstellingswijk:** One of many modernist structures created by Belgium's great 20th-century architect Léon Stynen, the BP Building is largely column-free and, as a result, home to an interior that's light and airy. The concrete block is supported by steel cables that hang from nine cross beams on its roof (in turn supported by two central beams).
162 Jan Van Rijswijcklaan, 2020

03 **Westkaai Towers, Eilandje:** It's hard to miss these six 17-storey residential blocks added during the 21st-century development of the Antwerp Docks. Basel studio Diener & Diener completed the two closest to the city with glass façades, while London-based Tony Fretton Architects designed the pair of simple brick towers that stand at the other end. David Chipperfield created the two towers in white concrete in between.
Kattendijkdok-Westkaai, 2000

③

Stadsschouwburg Antwerp,
Theaterbuurt
Fringe theatre

Built between 1968 and 1980,
Antwerp's municipal theatre
is commonly known as "the
concrete bunker". Two streets
(one badly bombed in 1944)
were cleared to make way for
a central square on which this
building was erected.

In 1974 a giant stained-glass
work of art by the Belgian artist
Herman Wauters was added
but it wasn't until 2008 that
the Stadsschouwburg was truly
transformed. A transparent
canopy supported by stick-thin
white columns was attached.
The slatted awning offers
protection from the rain while
letting through the light – the
perfect place to sip a drink
before taking in a show.
1 Theaterplein, 2000
+32 (0)3 400 5869
stadsschouwburg-antwerpen.be

I'm not lost, I'm just holding this for effect

④

Maison Guiette, Middelheim
Master of the home

Le Corbusier only erected
one permanent structure in
Belgium. Built for the artist
and critic René Guiette in
Antwerp's leafy southeastern
suburbs, Maison Guiette is a
compact encapsulation of the
great Swiss-French modernist's
sleek, astringent aesthetic.
Still a private residence, in
2016 it was listed as part of
the architect's Unesco World
Heritage site.

With a slim, tall profile,
Maison Guiette offers a
minimal, machine-like update
of a 19th-century Belgian
townhouse. Its concrete walls
rise to enclose a discrete roof
garden at the back, while
floor-to-ceiling windows on
the upper floor indicate
Guiette's studio.
32 Populierenlaan, 2020
fondationlecorbusier.fr

❺
Den Bell, Brederode
Building with buzz

Scottish engineer Graham Bell built the first foreign branch of the Bell Telephone Manufacturing Company in 1882 – and Belgian architect Hugo Van Kuyck added the jewel in the crown in 1958. At 13 stories high, Van Kuyck's modernist tower looms over the triangular complex of neo-renaissance buildings and contains a majestic staircase.

When the telephone company moved out in 2006, the council designated the site as the administrative centre of the city of Antwerp. Over the following years it renovated the space, turning the tower into a contemporary meeting centre, creating office spaces and carving out an inner courtyard that's open to the public.
1 Francis Wellesplein, 2018

Home visit
———
The 1958 former home and studio of Flemish architect Renaat Braem is a modernist marvel. Inspired by Le Corbusier, Braem created an open-plan structure with three glass façades to let in lots of light. Book a group tour with Expeditie De Stad.
expeditiedestad.be

Historical
Storied structures

❶
Amuz, Historisch Centrum
Building with front

It's not often that the foyer is as spectacular as the concert hall but that's certainly the case with Amuz. Here, guests mingle in a 19th-century winter chapel adorned with neo-Byzantine murals as they wait for the classical music to begin.

The hall itself, a former monastery of Augustinian friars, is also a sight to behold. Built between 1615 and 1618, it's a combination of architectural styles – the façade neo-renaissance and the interior baroque. Inside, the decor is original except for the three green-hued altarpieces created by Antwerp-based artist Jan Fabre in 2018, inspired by the Flemish masters but made from 450,000 beetles.
81 Kammenstraat, 2000
+ 32 (0)3 292 3680
amuz.be

②
Antwerpen-Centraal, Centraal
Station
Well travelled

Originally constructed between
1895 and 1905, Antwerpen-
Centraal replaced the original
terminus of the Brussels-
Mechelen-Antwerp railway.
It first welcomed trains in
1905 and today it's serviced
primarily by the Belgian
National Railway Company.

In the late 19th century the
Bruges-based architect Louis
Delacenserie transformed
what was once a lowly four-
track wooden shed into the
cathedral-like stone monument
it is today. Inspired by both
the station of Lucerne in
Switzerland and the Pantheon
in Rome, he created a structure
that's part neo-renaissance,
part art nouveau. It has a
striking waiting hall decked
with more than 20 kinds of
marble, arched windows and
a towering dome. Engineer
Clément Van Bogaert created
the train shed, with its vaulted
glass-and-steel roof.
27 Koningin Astridplein, 2018

③

Beguinage of Antwerp,
Universiteitsbuurt
Inner-city sanctuary

An oasis in the middle of the
city, the Beguinage is one of
Antwerp's secret treasures.
Behind a baroque doorway on
an otherwise unassuming side
street sits a tangle of cobbled
alleys and gabled houses,
redolent of a scene from an
early Dutch painting.

A characteristic feature
of medieval Flemish cities,
a *beguinage* is a home for lay
Catholic women. Although
there has been one in Antwerp
since 1240, the present
complex dates back to the
comparatively recent 1545.
It contains 45 apartments,
most of which are occupied
today, hidden behind narrow
wooden gates. Visitors are
welcome to explore and sit
in the verdant garden.
39 Rodestraat, 2000

④

Museum Plantin-Moretus,
Historisch Centrum
Prints charming

Font and print enthusiasts
would do well to visit this
Unesco World Heritage-listed
museum and former home
of master printer Christophe
Plantin. The 16th-century
mansion is full of some of
the world's oldest printing
presses and its library is lined
with 30,000 antique books
charting the finest examples
of typographic tradition.

The core part of the
creaky-floored complex was
constructed between 1576 and
1580, with four wings added in
three phases across the 16th,
17th and 18th centuries. Wend
your way through dimly lit
rooms before emerging into
a manicured inner garden.
22 Vrijdagmarkt, 2000
+32 (0)3 221 1450
museumplantinmoretus.be

City churches

01 Sint-Carolus
Borromeuskerk,
Historisch Centrum:
In a quiet square near
Grote Markt, this baroque
beauty was built between
1615 and 1621. Inspired
by Il Gesù, the Jesuit
church in Rome, Rubens
fashioned a highly
symmetrical façade with
neoclassical columns and
trumpet-tooting angels.
Before the fire of 1718,
after which the church
was rebuilt, the ceiling
was also lavishly covered
in paintings by Rubens.
carolusborromeus.com

02 Sint-Walburgiskerk,
Zuid: The original Sint-
Walburgiskerk dated
back to the 8th century,
when the first chapel
was created within its
walls. Rebuilt in the 14th
century, it became a
parish church in 1478
and in the 17th century
Rubens painted a triptych
for its high altar. In the
19th century the church
was demolished, and
in 1936 it was replaced
with a modernist church
by the same name.
41 Volkstraat, 2000

03 Kristus-Koningkerk,
Tentoonstellingswijk:
Designed by architect
Jos Smolderen as a
pavilion of religious
Flemish art for Antwerp's
1930 World Fair, the
modern Roman-Byzantine
Kristus-Koningkerk is a
cross-shaped basilica
with an interior of white
marble and brass.
Don't miss the sombre
sculptures by Alfons De
Roeck or Jos Michiels'
stained-glass windows.
*3 Louis Straussstraat,
2020*

Sport and fitness
── Exercise and the city

A little exercise won't go amiss after all the frites and chocolate. But don't worry, we won't be directing you towards a stuffy gym.

Instead we've sought out an open-air swimming spot, an art deco pool and plenty of green spaces for running and hiking – or just lazing on the grass with a good book if that's more your style. Plus, there's always the riverfront, where active residents flock on the weekends. And that's not to mention the cycling.

Water
Take the plunge

①
Boekenberg Swimming Pond,
Menegem
Eau naturelle

The word "pond" may not sound very appealing but bear with us. This open-air swimming complex is very much a pool – a long one too, at 73 metres – but it's totally natural and purified by the plant life on the bed.

Best of all, it's free to visit. (The season runs from mid-May to mid-September.) Note that skin-tight swimming suits are a must: no swim shorts. After you've had your fill of the water, explore Boekenbergpark, in which the pool is set.
68 Van Baurscheitlaan, 2100
+32 (0)3 411 1995
antwerpen.be

Wheel deal
──

Cyclant, next to Antwerpen-Centraal, offers a variety of rental bikes (including racers) for prolonged periods, as well as guided cycling tours of the city. Other rental services include Cloudbike, which can be accessed via its app.
cyclant.com; *cloudbike.be*

Ⓢ

Sportoase Veldstraat, Seefhoek
Swim in style

Public pools are a dime a dozen but it's not often you get to go for a dip in a 1930s art deco setting. The red-brick building – pastel-hued inside and delightfully symmetrical – has a pool, a hammam, a plunge pool and herbal baths.

Entry is €3 for adults. As with Boekenberg (*see opposite*), bikinis and loose swimming shorts are not allowed. The complex is slightly out of the way, especially if you're staying in the city centre, so consider cycling: there's a Velo station nearby on Stuivenbergplein.
83 Veldstraat, 2060
+ 32 (0)3 290 5555
sportoase.be/veldstraat

Parks
Go green

①

Park Spoor Noord, Den Dam
Open space

This park made headlines around Europe when it opened in 2009, partly because it injected life into a historically marginalised part of town.

Park Spoor Noord seemingly runs on forever, as bicycle lanes, running tracks, basketball courts, fountains and ample greenery unfold one after another. There's a large shallow pool for a quick wade and cool-down during summer. Once you've had your fill of exercise, head to Bar Noord – where you can kick back on sunloungers by a fountain – or Gå Nord for a bite to eat.
27 Damplein, 2060

Ⓢ

Rivierenhof, Deurne
Sunday stroll

This is Antwerp's Hyde Park or Bois de Boulogne: sprawling and with much to do. It opened in 1923 and has been a popular spot for Sunday outings for nigh-on a century. Walkers, cyclists and fishermen (there are plenty of ponds and lakes) can rejoice, as can history buffs, who shouldn't eschew a visit to Kasteel Sterckshof.

There are several food and drink options, including Kasteel Rivierenhof – a grand manor turned restaurant and bar. The easiest way to get here is by hopping on bus 410, which runs from near Antwerpen-Centraal (*see page 112*).
250 Turnhoutsebaan, 2100

Walk
—— Best foot
forward

Unlike Brussels, Antwerp
is a relatively compact
and walkable city. Most
of the cultural sights,
independent shops and
our favourite restaurants
and bars are within
walking distance of each
other. To give you an idea,
it takes just 15 minutes to
wander along the Schelde
from the 16th-century
Old Town to Eilandje, the
souped-up marina. And
if you tire of pounding
the pavement, you can
always hop on a bike.

Zurenborg and Haringrode
Good looks

The embellished façades of
Zurenborg townhouses attract
many to the streets of this
residential neighbourhood in
southeast Antwerp. At the end
of the 19th century the area
developed into a middle-class
enclave and, in the 1960s, it
escaped demolition thanks to a
campaign headed by celebrated
architect Renaat Braem. Over
the past few decades it has
gained popularity with families
and young professionals.

This walk begins across the
tracks in Haringrode, which
has benefitted from an overspill
of Zurenborg's popularity.
Start the walk hungry for both
tasty dishes and architectural
delights to best appreciate this
pocket of the city.

Architecture and fine food
Zurenborg and Haringrode walk

After sampling a pastry or
two at ❶ *Bakker Aldo*, wander
along Lange Leemstraat and
veer left into Groene Kwartier,
a residential development that
opened in a former military
hospital in 2010. Wend your
way around the leafy paths,
passing two-Michelin-starred
restaurant The Jane *(see page 75)*
in the centrally located chapel.

Opposite is Pakt *(see page
107)* and, inside, ❷ *Caffènation*,
which pioneered the coffee
revolution in Belgium in the
early 2000s. Grab an outdoor
table and enjoy a steaming cup
of coffee as you catch up on the
news. If tables are sparse, leave
Groene Kwartier and scoot
right onto Marialei. Here you'll
find ❸ *BarVert*, an airy corner
café with a pretty terrace.

Continue along Marialei,
popping into ❹ *The Plant
Corner* for a touch of greenery,

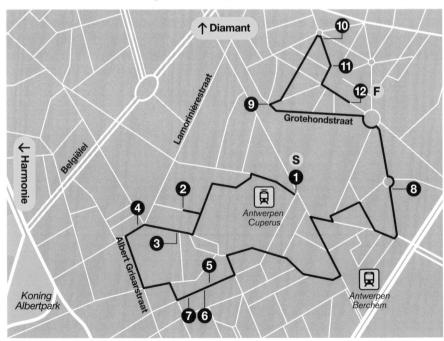

before leaning left onto Lamorinièrestraat. Take another left onto Albert Grisarstraat and at the end turn left again onto Boomgaardstraat. Veer right onto Bindstraat, then left onto Eikelstraat, and check out the jewellery and intricate woodwork at ⑤ *Zilver-Linde*.

Head back in the direction you came and brush up on some culture at ⑥ *Kunsthal Extra City* (*see page 100*) which hosts contemporary-art exhibitions and engaging talks. Then, give your legs a break with lunch next door at ⑦ *Extra Fika Eetcafé*, a café with a changing menu of seasonal dishes and plenty of vegetarian options.

Continue on Eikelstraat and turn left on Generaal Drubbelstraat. When you pass Frieterij Berchem, break right onto Boomgaardstraat, following the road around until you reach Stanleystraat, facing the train tracks. Zip left and walk away from Antwerpen-Berchem station before venturing down under the tracks on your right and arriving in Zurenborg.

Wander around the Generaal Van Merlenstraat and, at the junction, behold the four corner houses representing the four seasons, designed by Belgian architect Jos Bascourt in the art nouveau style. More awaits when you veer right onto Waterloostraat, turning left at the end and left again onto the famous ⑧ *Cogels-Osylei*

(*see page 109*). Take your time soaking up the façades of these grand mansions, which were designed in eclectic styles ranging from art nouveau to neo-gothic. At the end, curve around Draakplaats and take Grotehondstraat.

You'll pass Dôme, another Michelin-starred restaurant, and ⑨ *Domestic Bakkerij* on the corner opposite. Pick up a tartlet or sweet treat or, if you'd prefer to sit as you snack, continue along Arendstraat and take Grote Beerstraat to ⑩ *Walvis*, which is open for breakfast, lunch and aperitivos.

Hang around for nibbles or, if it's Belgian beer you're craving, continue to the heart of this neighbourhood: Dageraadplaats, the central square and a favourite hangout among residents. Enjoy *pintjes* at ⑪ *Moeskop*, dinner at Humm and end with a late-night cocktail at speakeasy ⑫ *Plantage*.

Address book

01 Bakker Aldo
388 Lange Leemstraat, 2018
+32 (0)3 239 2125
bakkeraldo.be

02 Caffènation
161 Lamorinièrestraat, 2018
+32 (0)3 501 2292
caffenation.be

03 Bar Vert
2 Helenalei, 2018
+32 (0)3 297 4188

04 The Plant Corner
144 Isabellalei, 2018
theplantcorner.com

05 Zilver-Linde
42 Eikelstraat, 2600
+32 (0)479 301 456
zilver-linde.be

06 Kunsthal Extra City
29 Eikelstraat, 2600
+32 (0)3 677 1655
extracitykunsthal.be

07 Extra Fika Eetcafé
25 Eikelstraat, 2600
+32 (0)498 331 934
extrafika.be

08 Cogels-Osylei
Cogels-Osylei, 2600

09 Domestic Bakkerij
37 Steenbokstraat, 2018
+32 (0)3 239 9890
domestic-bakkerij.be

10 Walvis
1 Walvisstraat, 2018
+32 (0)3 289 3322

11 Moeskop
17 Dageraadplaats, 2018
+32 (0)494 982 714

12 Plantage
28 Draakstraat, 2018
+32 (0)487 733 486

Best of the rest

Brussels and Antwerp may be the biggest cities in Belgium but the country has plenty of other patches worth perusing. Here are our tips for a handful of other cities we'd recommend you visit, all within easy striking distance of the capital.

①
Bruges
Off screen

Martin McDonagh's dark comedy *In Bruges* stars Colin Farrell and Brendan Gleeson as hitmen cooling off in the Flemish town after a botched job. The serenity of the cobbled streets, canals and medieval architecture soothes their consciences – and it's sure to soothe any affliction of yours too.

The city, whose name is thought to derive from the old-Scandinavian word for "harbour", is known for lace, castles and its postcard-perfect Unesco historic centre. Each day tourists pour from trains and coaches to marvel at the chocolate-box version of Old Europe, complete with gothic churches, quaint shops and lazy canal-boat trips.

Stroll the Peerdenbrug (Horse Bridge) past one of Belgium's oldest town halls, which was erected in 1421. Art-lovers should visit the Groeningemuseum, dedicated to six centuries of Flemish painting, and the 13th-century Church of Our Lady, home to a marble sculpture by Michelangelo – his only statue to have left Italy during his life.

2
Ghent
Family matters

A 30-minute train ride from the Belgian capital, this Flemish city exudes a fairytale charm with its ornate townhouses and cobbled streets. While Ghent is hardly undiscovered, it's less busy than Bruges. The smart restaurants, shops and cafés are just as likely to be frequented by students from the local university and well-heeled families who've called the city home for generations as day-trippers from Brussels or Antwerp.

"I wasn't planning to open a hotel in Ghent but in the next few years it will be the best city in this country," says Arnaud Zannier, owner of 1898 The Post. "It's a good mix: you've got students but also history. And we're in the Flemish heart so you've got lots of strong family businesses."

③
Liège
Striking structures

The French-speaking city
of Liège is easily reachable
from Brussels: trains run
from Bruxelles-Midi every
30 minutes and take an hour.
Once there, you'll find a
medieval, hilly town with plenty
of astounding architecture,
from imposing gothic churches
to contemporary wonders that
seem more suited for a major
capital – Liège-Guillemins train
station, for example, designed
by Santiago Calatrava.

Do visit Cathédrale Saint-
Paul de Liège, which has a
worldly collection of marble
statues including Guillaume
Geefs' "La génie du mal" (The
Genius of Evil), a sculpture of
Lucifer. Though itself sinisterly
beautiful, it was commissioned
to replace Geefs' brother's
attempt, which was deemed too
sexy for a depiction of Satan.

4

Leuven
School's out

This university town makes
for a great day trip from
Brussels. It's home to Belgium's
oldest university and the world's
largest brewing company (AB
InBev), as well as two charming
Unesco World Heritage-listed
beguinages (lay houses) and a
great art museum.

Granted, Leuven is slightly
overrun by students at night
but they tend to stick to Oude
Markt, one of the biggest bar-
lined squares in Europe. (Also,
if you come at the weekend
they'll have gone home).

Depending on your taste,
the soft smell of malt that
regularly wafts through the air
might put you off or get you
in the mood. Either way, order
yourself a cold Belgian beer
and perch at one of the alfresco
tables of the many fine bars
and restaurants.

Things we'd buy
── Take-away treats

We've shown you the top retail outposts across both cities, so hopefully you're well versed enough in the scene to bring back more than just *speculoos*. But we couldn't resist picking out a few items ourselves in between interviews, so allow us to give you a tip or two on what to take home.

Naturally there's a selection from Antwerp's fashion giants, including Dries Van Noten, and some sharp homeware items from the likes of Muller Van Severen. We've packed ceramics by an under-the-radar talent and more than one packet of biscuits to buoy any sinking spirits on the Eurostar. Plus Bruxellois stationery to pen your *pensées* and vintage Tintin for the little ones at home. On which note, we might need a second suitcase.

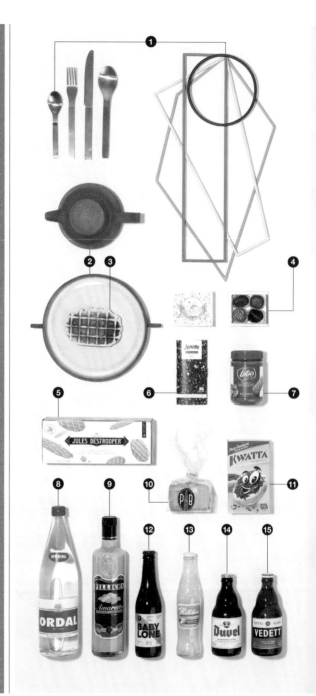

01 Muller Van Severen cutlery and trivets from Graanmarkt 13
graanmarkt13.com (Antwerp)
02 Alex Gabriels ceramics from St Vincents
stvincents.co (Antwerp)
03 Belgian waffle
(nationwide)
04 Chocolates by Mary
mary.be (Brussels)
05 Biscuits by Jules Destrooper
jules-destrooper.com
(nationwide)
06 Jerome chocolate from Native
native.bio (Antwerp)
07 *Speculoos* spread by Lotus Bakeries
lotusbakeries.com (nationwide)
08 Water by Ordal
(nationwide)
09 Jenever by Filliers
(nationwide)
10 Biscuits by Philip's Biscuits
philipsbiscuits.be (Antwerp)
11 Chocolate sprinkles by Kwatta
kwatta.be (nationwide)
12 Beer by Brussels Beer Project
beerproject.be (Brussels)
13 Lemonade by Ritchie
drinkritchie.com (nationwide)
14 Beer by Duvel
duvel.com (nationwide)
15 Beer by Vedett
vedett.com (nationwide)
16 Handbag by Lies Mertens
liesmertens.be (Antwerp)
17 Gloves by Ganterie Boon
glovesboon.be (Antwerp)
18 Bum bag and scarf by Bellerose
bellerose.be (Antwerp)
19 T-shirt by Dries Van Noten
driesvannoten.be (Antwerp)
20 Sunglasses by Komono
komono.com (Brussels)
21 Trainers by Maison Margiela
maisonmargiela.com (Brussels)
22 Howlin' socks from Morrison
morrison.be (Antwerp)

23 Vintage comics from
Marché aux Puces
marcheauxpuces.be (Brussels)
24 *Bruxelles à colorier* by
Gwen Guégan from Bozar
bozar.be (Brussels)
25 Letterpress letters from
Museum Plantin-Moretus
*museumplantinmoretus.be
(Antwerp)*

26 Notebooks by Le Typographe
typographe.be (Brussels)
27 *Henry Van de Velde: the Artist
as Designer* by Richard Hollis
and *Magritte, Broodthaers & L'Art
Contemporain* by Musées royaux
des Beaux-Arts de Belgique from
Peinture Fraîche
peinture-fraiche.be (Brussels)
28 Vinyl from Crevette Records
crevetterecords.be (Brussels)

6 essays
— Literary wanderings

What? Yes, of course dogs can read. No, this isn't just a prop

Belgian food love affair
Covert cookery

────

Think that Belgian cuisine can be summed up by beer, chocolate and chips? You just haven't been let in on the secret yet.

by Charlotte McDonald-Gibson, writer

High expectations are best left at home when it comes to many aspects of Belgian life. It's a down-to-earth place: showiness of the sort favoured across the border in France is frowned upon and if you want to make an impression less is always more. The best bars are often those with the simplest decor (think wooden tables and chairs); the best shops those with the plainest window displays. And when it comes to food, the same applies – Belgium likes to cloak its culinary charms from the average visitor, requiring some digging to discover its appeal.

When I arrived in Brussels in 2013, I wouldn't say I had high expectations of the cuisine – in fact, zero expectations might be more accurate. What did I know about Belgian food? The usual well-trod trio of beer,

chocolate and chips. While I was excited about the prospect of getting to know those strong, sweet ales, I was pretty ambivalent about the other two.

And so, after a few dry *carbonnade flamandes* (stews of beef cooked in beer) in the touristy areas, plus a plate or two of passable *moules-frites*, I figured I was done with my sampling of Belgian cuisine. But as the months passed, my new home slowly started to let me in on its gastronomic secrets.

A trip to De Groote Witte Arend, a traditional restaurant in Antwerp that specialises in pairing beers with local cuisine, revealed the extraordinary depth of flavour a brew can add to any meat. Chicken, beef, pork, game – all of them enhanced by a long, slow bath in a strong Belgian beer. Not long after, I discovered rabbit cooked in Kriek, a sour-cherry beer that proves the perfect match for the lean meat.

In winter these hearty stews are the most appealing meal you can imagine, especially when served at a cosy restaurant with an open fire in the Flemish countryside. Then, as the sun comes out, so does the Belgian gift for celebrating its produce. Across much of the country farmers have been growing the same crops for hundreds of years, meaning the Belgians have a knack for knowing exactly what will bring out the best in their yield. Chicory is tenderly wrapped in wafer-thin ham; asparagus is served with just the right amount of homemade egg mayonnaise; even the infamous brussels sprouts are brought to life with a pinch of grated nutmeg and lashings of butter.

Then there's the connection with the sea: Belgium's love of seafood stretches beyond the ubiquitous mussel (most of which are farmed in Zeeland in the Netherlands) to encompass elaborate platters of crustaceans and molluscs, many of them plucked from the North Sea and served with great fanfare at grand brasseries. For a simpler taste of the Belgian coast, sample its tiny, sweet grey prawns with a glass of Rodenbach beer.

While simplicity is at the heart of Belgian cuisine, there is a new generation of ambitious chefs putting its own twist on the national food – always with a focus on the produce. Belgium has one of the highest concentrations of Michelin stars per capita and you might even hear some of the capital's French residents whisper that the cuisine is better than that in Paris.

"Belgium likes to cloak its culinary charms from the average visitor, requiring some digging to discover its appeal"

So how do you find these culinary gems? As a rule, head to the places with the plain interiors; look for traditional dishes on the menu (my favourite restaurant in Brussels, Les Brasseries Georges, sometimes serves poached brains, enjoyed by a few Belgian grande dames with a dash of house mayonnaise); and order the specials, which make use of the most seasonal produce. If a place is packed at lunchtime, that's an excellent sign – the Belgians love a long lunch.

At its heart Belgian food is best home-cooked but if you can't scrounge an invite to a family dinner, it's surprisingly simple to master too. Before I left Brussels in 2018, I was given a cookbook called *The Taste of Belgium* and now it's my go-to tome whenever I want inspiration for cooking vegetables, or when autumn approaches and I can start thinking about which meat to stew in which beer again.

I have since moved next door to the Netherlands, which isn't exactly renowned for its food either. I keep hoping that in among all the fried and breadcrumbed balls of nondescript meat and the wheels of tasteless cheese, another secret cuisine is waiting to reveal itself. But somehow I doubt it. No one does hidden charm quite like the Belgians. — (M)

ABOUT THE WRITER: Charlotte McDonald-Gibson is a writer based in The Hague. From 2013 to 2018, she was MONOCLE's Brussels correspondent.

Watch your language
Linguistic lines in the sand

────

Doing the lingo limbo
is tricky in Belgium,
with multiple languages
and cultural sensitivities
aplenty. But no matter
who you're talking to,
there's one overriding rule:
never ask for French fries.

*by Charlotte Coussement,
writer*

First things first: Belgians don't speak "Belgian". Please, before you hop off the Eurostar, or disembark from the plane, rid this notion from your mind. And while we're on the subject, the same goes for French fries: there is no such thing. Fries are – and always will be – Belgian.

Misunderstandings such as these are fuelled by the fact that Belgium has no singular national narrative. Instead, I'm afraid, we like to complicate things. There are two main languages spoken here: Dutch, which we confusingly call Flemish, and French. (Officially, in fact, there are three: German is spoken by a tiny fraction in the east.) As a result, culture and customs can vary wildly from region to region.

One of the great question marks looming over greeting someone in Belgium is: to kiss or not to kiss? In French-speaking Wallonia, 90 per cent of residents *claque la bise* (kiss on the cheek), though just once, while in Dutch-speaking Flanders only 50 per cent do so. For French-speakers it's common to greet colleagues in the office with a quick peck. In Flanders such an act would attract funny looks.

At my Flemish primary school we had compulsory French lessons from age 10 until the end of high school, and since I was raised in a bilingual household I remember those classes being easy. Walloon pupils are also encouraged to learn a second language – Flemish, you might think. Actually they can choose any language, which in most cases ends up being English or German. In fact, the language divide has become so normal in daily life that a Flemish guy dating a French-speaking girl from the south will most likely simply converse in... English.

"The language divide also unites people; it's a core part of 'Belgitude' (the Belgian identity). Global events such as the World Cup and the Olympics are rare occasions when we don't distinguish between being Flemish or Walloon: we're Belgian"

Brussels is peculiar in its own right. Originally the capital was entirely Flemish-speaking but towards the end of the 18th century, after the occupation by France, its residents began to converse more commonly in French. Today the city continues to be mostly

French-speaking but it's surrounded by Flemish-language municipalities. As a result, it can be hard to tell whether the person beside you at a bar is *un Wallon* or *ne Vlaming*. Of course Flemish is still spoken in Brussels but, when it is, you might catch some eyes rolling.

Nevertheless, the language divide also unites people; it's a core part of *Belgitude* (the Belgian identity). Global events such as the World Cup and the Olympics are rare occasions when we don't distinguish between being Flemish or Walloon: we're Belgian. *Allez, les Belges!* City streets and cars are decked with Belgian flags. All of a sudden, we're no longer known as the country with political tensions: we're the French and Flemish who unite. Ironically, our patriotism shines through more on these sporting occasions than it does on Belgian National Day on 21 July – which, more than anything, is seen as a day to lie in and fire up the barbecue.

No matter what our mother tongue is, there are a few things we all have in common: a commitment to going for *pintjes* (small beers) in cafés, eating *pistolets* (sandwiches) on Sunday mornings and enjoying a love-hate relationship with the horrendous traffic jams during EU summits (we're proud that Brussels is in the spotlight for those couple of days but it comes at a price). Really, Belgians like to mix French and Flemish words – it's this blend that makes us who we are. We're aware that the world laughs at us. We laugh too. Yes, it's a bit of a muddle – but it's our muddle. — (M)

In order to prepare you for your time in Belgium, here are 10 words used in both French and Flemish (but derived from French) – i.e. everyone will understand you.

1. Frites: fries
2. Friterie: chip stand
3. Gazette: newspaper
4. Chouke: my darling (pronounced "shoeke")
5. Tournée générale: when a person treats the entire café to a beer
6. À l'improviste: to arrive unannounced/out of nowhere
7. Vélo: bicycle
8. Pistolet: typical Belgian bread roll eaten on Sunday morning. Crispy on the outside, soft on the inside
9. Maîtresse: mistress
10. Bonbon: candy

ABOUT THE WRITER: Charlotte Coussement was born and raised in the Belgian countryside near Brussels. She studied in London and Barcelona and – after a stint in the retail department at MONOCLE – now works as a freelance trend researcher.

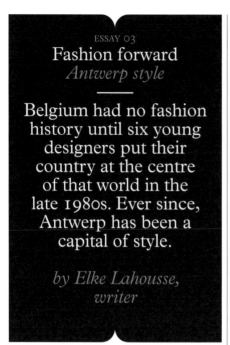

ESSAY 03

Fashion forward
Antwerp style

───

Belgium had no fashion history until six young designers put their country at the centre of that world in the late 1980s. Ever since, Antwerp has been a capital of style.

by Elke Lahousse, writer

I remember buying my first piece of designer clothing. I had just turned 25 and wanted to celebrate with a new outfit so I went to Het Modepaleis (The Fashion Palace), Dries Van Noten's beautiful shop in Antwerp. A few months earlier I had seen him present his summer 2009 ready-to-wear women's collection at the Palais Royal in Paris and I was blown away. Fashion shows can be more carnival than catwalk but here was a designer making clothes you could actually wear.

I bought a blue-and-orange silk top and matching silk trousers that faded from bright indigo to navy blue. Over the following few months I wore them exactly as they appeared on the catwalk, the top nonchalantly tucked into the waistband. I could never have imagined that more than 10 years later I would still be wearing them. I didn't know back then what I know now: that the shapes and cuts sprouting from Van Noten's creative mind are cleverly crafted and always flattering, without ever going out of style; and, more importantly, that no

other designer understands colour as well as him. My blue trousers have become more bewitching over the years, the perfect antidote to the grey Belgian weather.

The refusal to follow mainstream trends and whims is a characteristic that unites a number of Belgian designers. Instead of experimenting with extreme cuts or bold volumes – still the norm in contemporary fashion – many devote their career to a single vision, season after season, as if writing chapter after chapter of the same book. Ann Demeulemeester, for example, spent years experimenting with the countless possibilities of black, calling it the most poetic colour. (She left her label in 2013, announcing that Ann Demeulemeester was an adult brand now, but the company continues to keep her vision, and her love of black, alive.)

Belgian fashion is a relatively recent thing. It all began in 1986 when a small group of graduates from Antwerp's Royal Academy of Fine Arts squeezed themselves and their collections into the back of a van

and drove to London to attend the British Designer Show. They were offered a stand on the top floor, between the bridal gowns, where no buyers ventured because all the bigger designers were showing on the first floor – that is, until someone from Barneys in New York passed by. A tsunami of buyers, agents and press followed and the Belgian designers returned home with multiple orders. From London they went to Paris, where they had their own fashion shows, and gradually they put Belgium at the centre of the fashion world. Their names? Dries Van Noten, Ann Demeulemeester, Walter Van Beirendonck, Dirk Van Saene, Marina Yee and Dirk Bikkembergs. The English press had difficulties pronouncing those long Flemish names and promptly labelled them "the Antwerp Six".

People still refer to the Antwerp Six as an untouchable group no one will ever be able to match, which of course isn't the case. Abroad the media licked its lips over the story of the Six, portraying them as a group of steadfast friends, but in Belgium the designers did everything possible to mark their individuality. In their own unique ways they have continuously tried to further Belgian fashion – and the likes of Christian Wijnants, Stephan Schneider, Kris Van Assche, Haider Ackermann and Demna Gvasalia have followed. All of the above are alumni from the fashion department of Antwerp's Royal Academy of Fine Arts, one of the most dynamic and renowned fashion schools in the world, attracting students from more than 40 different nationalities.

"The refusal to follow mainstream trends unites a number of Belgian designers. Instead of experimenting with extreme cuts or bold volumes many devote their career to a single vision"

Van Beirendonck is now head of the fashion department and watchdog of the academy's experimental ethos.

No one can deny that the Six, together with the city's flourishing fashion school, have made Antwerp a more exciting place over the past 30 years. Walk along streets such as Nationalestraat or Steenhouwersvest and you will find Momu, Antwerp's fashion museum, next to high-end vintage shops and various stores pursuing an avant garde profile. Its vibrant fashion scene was one of the reasons I moved to Antwerp; I love the fact that many Belgian designers continue to live and work in the city instead of moving to parallel fashion universes such as London, Paris or Tokyo. I once had the pleasure of strolling through Antwerp's tiny botanical garden with Van Noten, who told me about his love of "ugly" flowers. Ever since I've enjoyed imagining him escaping his busy studio in Eilandje from time to time and riding his bike to see what's in bloom.

The seismic shifts that the fashion industry has undergone in recent years have naturally influenced Belgium's fashion scene but the collections that our designers put out remain an export to be proud of. So, when planning your trip to Antwerp, try to visit during the first week of May or November when the designer stock sales take place. It's a great opportunity to add some of that Van Noten blue or Demeulemeester black to your wardrobe at a bargain price – and a souvenir that will give you great pleasure for years to come. — (M)

ABOUT THE WRITER: Elke Lahousse is a journalist at *Knack Weekend*, Belgium's oldest lifestyle magazine. During her years as its fashion reporter she mostly enjoyed interviewing Belgian designers. She moved to Antwerp in 2015.

ESSAY 04

Face value
Brussels' bad rap

———

Don't let the plethora
of politicians fool
you – there's plenty to
discover in the Belgian
capital beyond the
EU, as our assistant
editor discovered.

*by Melkon Charchoglyan,
Monocle*

When I was at university, most of the people I knew were jetting off to exotic places such as Sardinia, Morocco or the West Coast of the US. I went to Brussels. I can't remember what the thinking behind that decision was but I do remember the derision and strange silence when I told my peers. "Brussels," they said. "Are you going for an internship or something?" No, very much a holiday. Cue tight-lipped smile.

Admittedly, Brussels was a rogue choice. It has a terrible reputation and we all know why: the European Union. The EU coming to Brussels was about as good for its street cred as your mum picking you up after a night out. It's not so much the political weight of the institution as its all-consuming and transient nature. Thousands of politicians, attachés, clerks and administrative small-fry descend on the city from Monday to Friday, engulfing current affairs and all conversation. Come Saturday they disappear and the Quartier Européen falls silent, like New York's Wall Street or London's Canary Wharf out of

hours. To the untrained eye, it can seem as though Brussels is just one great big office, bereft of any personality once the politicians have flown home.

I won't lie – Brussels didn't blow my mind when I first visited as a student, perhaps because I saw little beyond the crocheted window of a dark pub, stumbling from Leffe to Leffe, my mouth smeared with free chocolate samples. On my return home, everyone said the same thing: "Of course it was boring. It's Brussels!" But I wasn't so sure. I felt that I'd missed something; the city's spirit had eluded me (or rather I'd failed to discover it.) I made the error that most visitors fall foul to: I didn't leave the centre of town.

Brussels is a city that rewards the curious and the active. It's not a dense, sardine tin of experiences like other major cities around the world. The Belgian capital is slower, more nuanced, its pay-offs more dispersed. When the opportunity came to return to Brussels for this guide and explore the city properly, I relished it.

My key advice to any visitor is to walk everywhere and explore the suburbs. Brussels' rich history and character are played out in these peripheral patches, and each one has a distinct personality.

Take Flagey for example. The focal point of this lively neighbourhood is the main square, Place Eugène Flagey, which sits around two bodies of water that lend the area a pleasantly provincial feel. One evening my colleagues and I had the Syrian dinner of our lives here, grabbed a beer in a retro bar and then noshed frites well past our bedtime on the square. The day after we returned for arguably the best pizza I've tried outside Italy. Were we in Brussels? We were having too good a time.

Then there's Saint-Gilles. Oh, sweet Saint-Gilles. Bruxellois expats often say that the city is one for living, not visiting. While not entirely true, it does hold currency in this particular neighbourhood. The pace of life is slower, the bars more numerous, their tables spilling out to the very edge of the pavement. Add to this pretty tree-lined streets, trams

"One evening my colleagues and I had the Syrian dinner of our lives here, grabbed a beer in a retro bar and then noshed frites well past our bedtime on the square. The day after we returned for arguably the best pizza I've tried outside Italy. Were we in Brussels? We were having too good a time"

that shuffle by at old-world speeds, farmers' markets, hidden art galleries and a carousel of jaw-dropping art nouveau architecture at every corner – and, well, you can see why it's an appealing place to live.

The greatest surprise of them all is Molenbeek. The area has been villainised in the press as a hotbed of terrorism but it was here that I stumbled across a party that made me want to miss my train back to London. On a Saturday night an organisation called Recyclart had put together an enormous warehouse rave to celebrate its new venue. Hundreds of revellers drank pale ale and danced to electronic music; everyone seemed to know each other, and the amiable atmosphere suggested that this night was not a novelty but business as usual. Recyclart has a huge remit: among other things, it stages art exhibitions, arranges carpentry workshops, runs a bar and restaurant, and generally engages with the local community to build a more prosperous Brussels. Such movements are not an anomaly here. They fly under the radar, eclipsed by the capital's unjustly bland reputation, but to me this made them even more sexy and desirable.

With our time in Brussels coming to an end, I felt that I'd personally only scratched the surface of this city. On the last day somebody told me that the area around Bruxelles-Midi – historically a place to be avoided – was on the up, and that the nightlife was moving here. Clearly there was much more to discover.

By all means, take selfies with the Manneken Pis, ogle flowers on the Grand Place and drink coffee in the Galleries, but keep a curious disposition and explore widely if you'd really like to get to the heart of this city. Don't expect to be the only one with a nose on the scent, though; the secret seems to be out. Just the other day, mulling over a weekend away, a friend of mine said, "I hear Brussels is nice." — (M)

ABOUT THE WRITER: Melkon Charchoglyan is MONOCLE's assistant Books editor. For this guide, he roamed all over Brussels to discover its finest architecture and then pondered where's best to stay in Antwerp – which involved a lot of evenings spent in hotel bars.

ESSAY 05
Shock of the new
City beats

———

The electronic music scenes in Brussels and Antwerp have emerged out of the underground and into the light, thanks to a dedicated and eclectic crew of industry insiders.

by Nicholas Lewis, writer

"Those involved began to recognise that more could be achieved if they managed to rise above their purist sensibilities"

Since 2015, Brussels and Antwerp have witnessed a renaissance in their electronic music scenes. This has been driven by a prolific and committed ecosystem of musicians, labels, venues, festivals and streaming platforms all working towards one goal – to give Belgium's music landscape the professional framework it deserves.

I remember a time when the communications guy from a certain label used to hand-deliver promo copies of its latest releases to me by bicycle. Some might say – and I count myself in this tribe – that those were the days, when relationships were developed face-to-face with a handshake, as opposed to through social media with a click and a like. But that kind of hyper-localised communications strategy had its limitations and could only go so far in furthering the interests of the artists whose music warranted a wider audience.

The problem with both cities' electronic scenes back then was simply that they lacked professionalism. Music was created out of sheer passion and an unwavering belief in the economy of the underground; constructing a career out of your art – at least for the tight-knit crew of bands, solo musicians and producers active then – was often a secondary, if not non-existent, end game. Fragmentation was also an issue, with too many collectives, labels, promoters and venues working in their own isolated circles but rarely coming together. The content, substance and output were there but no one other than the truly initiated knew it.

That all changed when those involved began to recognise that more could be achieved if they managed to rise above their purist sensibilities and very Belgian tendencies for self-effacement. Brussels-based record label Vlek – with its laser-like focus on left-field electronic musicians who had grown up on a mix of alternative hip hop and, well, Aphex Twin – undoubtedly helped to pave the way. Meanwhile, in Antwerp, Ekster began churning out an impeccably curated discography of releases too, putting the city's then little-known electronic-inclined musicians on the map. An unwavering support of local talent was – and remains – a core component of each imprint, which in itself helped to nurture fervent homegrown scenes and inspire offspring – JJ Funhouse, Le Pacifique Records, Stroom and Basic Moves to name a few.

Live-music venues have always played a vital role in the maturation of Belgium's music scene. Les Ateliers Claus, Recyclart and Beursschouwburg in Brussels – as well as Het Bos in Antwerp, Vooruit in Ghent and Stuk in Leuven – gave talent a stage on which to shine, introducing audiences to emerging artists spanning countless genres by booking them as opening acts to their more established counterparts. These cultural

institutions and venues also excelled in acting as platforms for a heady mix of party promoters and festival organisers, with Beursschouwburg doing a particularly commendable job of crafting a unique voice for itself through its eclectically genial programme while trusting other, often more niche, concepts to take over certain nights.

On the festival front, the coming-of-age of Belgium's electronic music landscape has much to owe to the organisers who have made it their mission to elevate the scene. In Brussels, Bozar Electronic Arts Festival is a clear contender for its pioneering spirit, while newcomers such as Listen! Festival (the winner-takes-all fiesta that has single-handedly brought an Amsterdam Dance Event vibe to town) and Schiev (the lovable, humble and experimental option) have also done a tremendous job of reinvigorating the local fabric.

And last but not least, a slew of new online radio stations have also played their part. We Are Various (nestled in the café of Fomu, Antwerp's museum for photography), Kiosk Radio (an online community radio hosted from, you've guessed it, a wooden kiosk in the Parc de Bruxelles) and The Word Radio (a streaming and content platform with more experimental and exploratory inclinations that I launched in 2017 together with Quentin Materne) have all mastered advances in audio and video streaming technology to give a more approachable and immersive experience to listeners.

All in all, there's really never been a better time to be both musician and music fan in Belgium. — (M)

ABOUT THE WRITER: Nicholas Lewis is the co-founder of The Word Radio station. He was born in Brussels, where he still lives with his partner, son and ever-growing record collection.

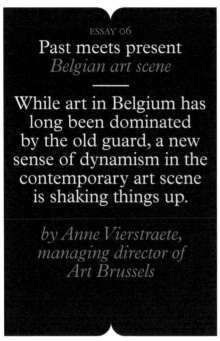

Past meets present
Belgian art scene

While art in Belgium has long been dominated by the old guard, a new sense of dynamism in the contemporary art scene is shaking things up.

by Anne Vierstraete, managing director of Art Brussels

Think of art in Belgium and you'd be forgiven for feeling stumped after picturing the wacky works of surrealist René Magritte and Hubert and Jan Van Eyck's famous Ghent altarpiece. Belgium is a country rich in artistic heritage, from the Flemish baroque (best represented by the great Peter Paul Rubens) to the ginger-haired boy we call Tintin. It's also, however, making a name for itself on the international contemporary art scene.

To come to Belgium and bypass its artistic heritage would, of course, be unimaginable – and near impossible since the imprint of the past is ever present. Savour the historic Belgian spirit in Bruges, one of the best-preserved examples of a medieval city centre in Europe with its magical ensemble of cobblestone paths, brick archways, stone churches and quaint bridges. Brussels too has a historical heart – the Grand Place, an exceptional jewel of 17th-century architecture rebuilt after the bombing by the French army in 1695 and designated a Unesco World Heritage site in 1998. And over in Antwerp there's the exceptional Rubenshuis, where the prominent Flemish painter lived with his family and painted alongside colleagues and assistants.

A visit to Belgium isn't complete without an exploration of the cultural delights created by the old-guard artists for which it's known. In Ghent you can admire one of the most important paintings in western art: the "Adoration of the Mystic Lamb" by the brothers Hubert and Jan Van Eyck. Jan is said to have completed the Ghent altarpiece in 1432, a few years after his older brother's death, conveying pictorial details through the masterful use of oil paint. Back in Brussels, seek out the landscape and peasant scenes by Pieter Bruegel the Elder at both the Musées Royaux des Beaux-Arts de Belgique and the Bibliothèque Royale, then delve into the weird and wonderful world of the Brussels-based René Magritte. By 1924, Belgium – like France – had initiated a surrealist scene that prioritised the creative process over the final piece.

It was during the second half of the 20th century that Belgium started to shine a spotlight on contemporary art. In 1968 – just a year after Cologne launched Kölner Kunstmarkt, the first contemporary art fair in the world –

11 Belgian gallerists established a comparable event that set the premise for Art Brussels, now one of Europe's most renowned contemporary art fairs. Seven years later the city of Ghent opened the first Belgian museum devoted to contemporary art, which was renamed Smak in 1999 and swiftly became known for its avant garde programme. And in 2007, Brussels too became home to a leading institution for contemporary art when Wiels opened its doors in a restored brewery with a roster of temporary exhibitions by national and international artists, both emerging and established.

"To come to Belgium and bypass its artistic heritage would, of course, be unimaginable – and near impossible since the imprint of the past is ever present"

Commercial galleries also play a vital role in the contemporary-art landscape. In Brussels they're largely grouped by neighbourhood and often occupy big, beautiful spaces – ideal environments in which to view art. Antwerp too has a whole host of galleries housed in extraordinary buildings worthy of the works within. Must-visits include the internationally renowned Zeno X – which represents some of Belgium's most famous contemporary artists such as Luc Tuymans and Michael Borremans – and Axel Vervoordt Gallery, located in the architecturally astounding Kanaal, the former industrial complex along the Albert Canal in Wijnegem. Belgium is home to a plethora of artistic treasures that are not always easy to find. So one of the best times to explore the country's contemporary art scene is during Art Brussels, which takes place every year in the second half of April. Considered a highlight in the international cultural calendar, this week-long fair sees Brussels' galleries, as well as private and public institutions, open their most important exhibitions of the year. It also provides a nice contrast for those hoping to explore the more historical assets of the city and further afield.

The enthusiasm Belgians feel towards both their artistic heritage and contemporary-art production is infectious – and not unlike the pride they feel when it comes to their nation's culinary scene. Of course, another thing you can't miss during your visit to Belgium is a trip to one of our traditional *friterie*. But that's another story. — (M)

ABOUT THE WRITER: Anne Vierstraete has run Art Brussels since August 2013. In 2017, she was at the helm of the celebrations for the 50th anniversary of the fair, marking the significant role it has played in the burgeoning art scene in Belgium.

Resources
—— Brussels

Soundtrack to the city
Listen up

01 **César Franck, 'Violin Sonata in A Major' (1886):** Composed in Franck's twilight years as a wedding present for friend and fellow Belgian violinist Eugène Ysaÿe.

02 **Jacques Brel, 'Ne me quitte pas' (1959):** Arguably the greatest and certainly the most popular song by Jacques Brel, who is nothing short of a national treasure in Belgium.

03 **Toots Thielemans, 'Bluesette' (1961):** A soulful number by the godfather of the Belgian jazz tradition.

04 **Stromae, 'Alors on danse' (2009):** Catchy title that combines hip-hop and electro dance.

Transport
Getting here

01 **Eurostar:** Regular Eurostar services link Brussels to London, Paris and Amsterdam. *eurostar.com*

02 **Flying:** Aéroport de Bruxelles-National links to 164 destinations. The train from the airport to Bruxelles-Central station takes 17 minutes and costs €8.90. A taxi to the centre costs about €45. *brusselsairport.be*

Transport
Getting around

01 **Tram and metro:** Brussels' extensive tram network has 17 lines, the metro six. Tickets, which can be purchased at metro stations, are valid on both. A single journey costs €2.10; a five-journey pass sets you back €8. *stib-mivb.be*

02 **Taxi:** Taxis here are some of the most expensive in Europe. Though the base fare is €2.40, the per-kilometre charge is between €1.80 and €2.70.

03 **Bike:** The yellow Villo! bikes are available for hire from 360 docking stations around town. Register online and download the app to use them. A €1.60 pass allows you to use Villo! for 24 hours; the first 30 minutes of every journey are free with an incremental charge thereafter. *villo.be*

Vocabulary
Tip of the tongue

01 **Coucou:** hello (informal)
02 **Une chope:** a beer
03 **Dikkenek:** someone arrogant or pretentious
04 **Zievereir:** joker
05 **Allons-y!** let's go!
06 **Dada!** bye!

Best events
What, where, when

01 **BRAFA Art Fair, Tours & Taxis:** This event has been running since 1956 and exhibits everything from antiques to fine art. *January/February, brafa.art*

02 **Art Brussels, Tours & Taxis:** The contemporary-art fair gathers some 180 international galleries. *April, artbrussels.com*

03 **Brussels Jazz Weekend, citywide:** Three days of free concerts, from swing to bebop. *May, brusselsjazzweekend.be*

04 **Europe Day, Quartier Européen:** Activities, talks and tours of EU buildings such as the Bâtiment Europa (*see page 48*). *May, europa.eu*

05 **Brussels Independent Film Festival, citywide:** A film festival with emphasis on indie productions. *June, brusselsfilmfestival.com*

06 **Flower Carpet, Grand Place:** Every two years the square is covered in a million begonias. *August, brussels.be/flower-carpet*

07 **Brussels Summer Festival, citywide:** Ten days of concerts and events around the city. *August, bsf.be*

08 **Design September, citywide:** A celebration of design with conferences, exhibitions and debates around town. *September, designseptember.be*

09 **Winter Wonders, citywide:** Christmas markets, pageants and processions. *November to January, plaisirsdhiver.be*

Resources
—— Antwerp

Best of Belgian literature
By the book

01 Georges Simenon, 'The Stain on the Snow' (1948): A dark, psychological thriller from one of the masters of Belgian storytelling.

02 Marguerite Yourcenar, 'Memoirs of Hadrian' (1951): Yourcenar's fictional memoir of the Roman emperor.

03 Hugo Claus, 'The Sorrow of Belgium' (1938): Set in Belgium during the Second World War, this is considered one of the country's greatest Dutch-language novels.

Transport
Getting here

01 Train: Antwerpen-Centraal is conveniently located in the city centre, as the name attests. Trains to Brussels run more or less every 30 minutes and take 45 minutes to an hour, depending on which of the capital's stations you hop off at.
belgianrail.be

02 Airport: Antwerp only has a small airport that services 14 destinations. If you do fly in, a taxi (which costs about €15 and takes 15 minutes) is the best way of getting to the city.
antwerp-airport.com

Transport
Getting around

01 Bike: Everyone cycles in Antwerp and the city has built an extensive network of bike routes. The easiest way to get involved is by using the Velo Antwerpen bike-share scheme, which has hundreds of stations around town. Register online and off you go.
velo-antwerpen.be

02 Tram and metro: Antwerp has a widespread electric tram system that also, in parts, runs underground. A single ticket, valid for an hour, costs €3, while a day pass is €7 and can be bought from machines at every station or mini-marts such as Albert Heijn. (As in Brussels, these tickets are also valid on the bus.)
delijn.be

03 Taxis: Taxis are generally not necessary in Antwerp as the city is walkable and has good public transport. If you do require one, hail it on the street (they have red plates) or order one via the Taxi.eu app.
taxi.eu

Vocabulary
Language lessons

01 Een pintje: half-pint of the lager on draft
02 Dankjewel: thank you
03 De rekening, alstublieft: the bill please
04 Nachtwinkel: nightshop
05 T' stad: the city (as referred to Antwerp)
06 Velookes: the Velo Antwerpen city bikes

Best events
Dates for the diary

01 Antwerp Poster Festival, Pakt, citywide: A nascent, several-day event promoting graphic design talent from around the world.
March, apf.design

02 Antwerp Art Weekend, citywide: Gallerists from all over Europe descend on Antwerp for four days, plus museums put on special events.
May, antwerpart.com

03 Bierpassie Weekend, Groenplaats: Scores of stalls sell beer from across Belgium, accompanied by appropriately kitsch brass brands.
June, bierpassieweekend.be

04 Tomorrowland, Boom: One of the biggest dance festivals in the world takes place in a town just outside Antwerp.
July, tomorrowland.com

05 Rubens Market, Historisch Centrum: The historic centre is transformed into a 17th-century market, with stalls selling everything from fruit to flowers, and vendors dressed in traditional garb.
15th August

06 Jazz Middelheim, Park Den Brandt: A fixture of Europe's jazz calendar with four days of jazz and blues.
August, jazzmiddelheim.be

07 Antwerp Christmas Market, Grote Markt: A celebration of the festive season and the best Antwerp has to offer: expect regional goodies aplenty.
December

About Monocle
—— Step inside

London HQ
Our editorial office is in Marylebone

In 2007, Monocle was launched as a monthly magazine briefing on global affairs, business, culture, design and much more. We believed there was a globally minded audience of readers who were hungry for opportunities and experiences beyond their national borders.

Today Monocle is a complete media brand with print, audio and online elements – not to mention our expanding network of shops and cafés. Besides our London HQ we have international bureaux in Toronto, Tokyo, Zürich, Hong Kong and Los Angeles, with more on the way. We continue to grow and flourish and at our core is the simple belief that there will always be a place for a print brand that is committed to telling fresh stories and sending photographers on assignments. It's also a case of knowing that our success is all down to the readers, advertisers and collaborators who have supported us along the way.

❶
International bureaux
Boots on the ground

We're based in London and have bureaux in Hong Kong, Tokyo, Zürich, Toronto and Los Angeles, with more to come. We also call upon reports from our contributors in more than 35 cities around the world. For this guide, MONOCLE reporters Joe Pickard, Chloë Ashby, Melkon Charchoglyan and Joleen Goffin decamped to Brussels and Antwerp to explore all they have to offer. They also met with various contacts to ensure that we've covered the best in food, culture and more.

❷
Online
Digital delivery

We have a dynamic website: *monocle.com.* As well as being the place to hear our radio station, Monocle 24, the site presents our films, which are beautifully shot and edited by our in-house team and provide a fresh perspective on our stories. Check out the films celebrating the cities that make up our Travel Guide Series before you explore the rest of the site.

❸
Retail and cafés
Food for thought

Via our shops in Hong Kong, Toronto, Zürich, Tokyo, London and Los Angeles we sell products that cater to our readers' tastes and are produced in collaboration with brands we believe in. We also have cafés in Tokyo, Zürich and London. And if you are in the UK capital visit the Kioskafé in Paddington, which combines good coffee and great reads.

4 Print
Committed to the page

MONOCLE is published 10 times a year. We also produce two standalone publications – THE FORECAST, packed with insights into the year ahead, and THE ESCAPIST – plus seasonal weekly newspapers and an annual *Drinking & Dining Directory*. Since 2013 we have also been publishing books, like this one, in partnership with Gestalten. Visit *monocle.com/shop*.

5 Radio
Sound approach

Monocle 24 is our round-the-clock radio station that was launched in 2011. It delivers global news and shows covering foreign affairs, urbanism, business, culture, food and drink, design and print media. When you find yourself in Belgium, tune into *The Globalist* for a newsy start to your morning. You can listen live or download any of our shows from *monocle.com*, iTunes or SoundCloud.

Join the club

01
Subscribe to Monocle
A subscription is a simple way to make sure that you never miss an issue – and you'll enjoy many additional benefits.

02
Be in the know
Our subscribers have exclusive access to the entire Monocle archive, and priority access to selected product collaborations, at *monocle.com*.

03
Stay in the loop
Subscription copies are delivered to your door at no extra cost no matter where you are in the world. We also offer an auto-renewal service to ensure that you never miss an issue.

04
And there's more...
Subscribers benefit from a 10 per cent discount at all Monocle shops, including online, and receive exclusive offers and invitations to events around the world.

Choose your package

Premium one year
13 × issues
+ Porter Sub Club bag

One year
12 × issues
+ Monocle Voyage tote bag

Six months
6 × issues

Writers
Chloë Ashby
Melkon Charchoglyan
Charlotte Coussement
Madévi Dailly
Koen Galle
Nolan Giles
Joleen Goffin
Clodagh Kinsella
Elke Lahousse
Nicholas Lewis
Joe Lloyd
Charlotte McDonald-Gibson
Debbie Pappyn
Joe Pickard
Anne Vierstraete

Research
Natalie Chalk
Gabriele Dellisanti
Audrone Fiodorenko
Zayana Zulkiflee

Special thanks
Lien Annicaert
Jozefien Van Beek
Nuria Bellido
City of Antwerp
Lior Cohen
Georgina Godwin
Tom Hall
Irene Hua
Lewis Huxley
Pierre Massart
Debbie Pappyn
Rosie Prata
Louise Przybylski
Thomas Reynolds
Audrey Schayes
Joseph Spinks
Thomas Verschuren
Martin Vigren
Visit Brussels
Harry Wong
Sebastiaan Wouters

PICTURES: BRUSSELS

Chief photographer
Jussi Puikkonen

Still life
David Sykes

Photographer
Ben Clement

Images
Alamy
Melkon Charchoglyan
Getty Images
Paul Louis
Veerle Vercauteren

Illustrators
Satoshi Hashimoto
Ceylan Sahin
Kouzou Sakai
Tokuma

PICTURES: ANTWERP

Chief photographer
David De Vleeschauwer

Still life
David Sykes

Images
Hufton+Crow
Carlos Montero-Caballero
Joe Pickard

Illustrators
Satoshi Hashimoto
Ceylan Sahin
Kouzou Sakai
Tokuma

Monocle
EDITOR IN CHIEF AND
CHAIRMAN
Tyler Brûlé
EDITOR
Andrew Tuck
CREATIVE DIRECTOR
Richard Spencer Powell

**The Monocle Travel Guide
Series: Brussels + Antwerp**
GUIDE EDITOR
Chloë Ashby
ASSOCIATE GUIDE EDITORS
Melkon Charchoglyan
Joleen Goffin
Joe Pickard
PHOTO EDITOR
Victoria Cagol

**The Monocle Travel Guide
Series**
SERIES EDITOR
Joe Pickard
ASSOCIATE EDITOR
Chloë Ashby
ASSISTANT EDITOR
Melkon Charchoglyan
DESIGNER
Giulia Tugnoli
PHOTO EDITOR
Victoria Cagol

CHAPTER EDITING: BRUSSELS

Need to know
Melkon Charchoglyan

🅗 ❶
Hotels
Chloë Ashby

🅕 ❷
Food and drink
Madévi Dailly

🅡 ❸
Retail
Joleen Goffin

🅒 ❹
Culture
Chloë Ashby

🅓 ❺
Design and architecture
Melkon Charchoglyan

🅢 ❻
Sport and fitness
Joe Pickard

🅦 ❼
Walk
Melkon Charchoglyan

CHAPTER EDITING: ANTWERP

🅜
Need to know
Melkon Charchoglyan

🅗 ❶
Hotels
Melkon Charchoglyan

🅕 ❷
Food and drink
Clodagh Kinsella

🅡 ❸
Retail
Joe Pickard

🅒 ❹
Culture
Joleen Goffin

🅓 ❺
Design and architecture
Chloë Ashby

🅢 ❻
Sport and fitness
Melkon Charchoglyan

🅦 ❼
Walk
Joleen Goffin

🅜
Essays
Chloë Ashby

🅜
Things we'd buy
Melkon Charchoglyan
Joe Pickard

🅜
Resources
Melkon Charchoglyan

The MONOCLE *Travel Guide Series* 34

Athens

... Kalimera! Stroll with us through the city's outposts of good food, design, retail and more. Pame! ...

The MONOCLE *Travel Guide Series* 35

Helsinki

... Moi! Dive into the city's outposts of good food, design, retail and more. Hello, calmis? ...

New

The collection

Planning another trip? We have a global suite of guides, with more set to be released. Cities are fun. Let's explore.

The MONOCLE *Travel Guide Series* 36

Hamburg

... Moin moin! Hop aboard for a tour of the city's best outposts in good food, design, retail and more. Gute Reise! ...

The MONOCLE *Travel Guide Series* 37

Chicago

... Race with us through the city's outposts of good food, design, retail and more. On your marks! ...

Buy today at all good bookshops

You can also visit the online shops at *monocle.com* and *shop.gestalten.com* to get hold of your copies.

Look out for 'The Monocle Guide to Hotels, Inns and Hideaways'